yummy supper

yummy supper

100 Fresh, Luscious & Honest Recipes
from a {Gluten-Free} Omnivore

Erin Scott

RODALE

© 2014 by Erin Scott

Photographs © 2014 by Erin Scott

Rodale books may be purchased for business or promotional use or for special sales. For information, please write to:
Special Markets Department, Rodale, Inc., 733 Third Avenue, New York, NY 10017

Printed in the United States of America

Rodale Inc. makes every effort to use acid-free ⊗, recycled paper ♺.

Book design by Kara Plikaitis

Library of Congress Cataloging-in-Publication Data is on file with the publisher.

ISBN-13: 978-1-60961-544-4

Distributed to the trade by Macmillan

2   4   6   8   10   9   7   5   3   1   paperback

We inspire and enable people to improve their lives and the world around them.
rodalebooks.com

for Paul, Otis, and Lilah—
loves of my life

table of contents

fruit

kid favorites

odds + ends

disclaimer

I write this book as a passionate home cook and mother living with celiac disease and am not a medical professional. Any suggestions I make about gluten-free eating are from my own personal experience and are not intended as a medical directive. If you are looking for medical information about celiac disease or non-celiac gluten intolerance, please consult your doctor or health-care practitioner.

introduction

Fish tacos with pomegranate salsa tucked into warm corn tortillas, happily made from scratch by the kiddos. Homemade crème fraîche. Rainbow slaw packed with purple cabbage, green apple, radish, and orange. A pot of smoky Midnight black beans. Watermelon punch with fresh lime and crushed mint. This is supper at our house. Friends chat, kids play, and we eat simple goodness. I don't think you would ever guess that our kitchen is 100 percent gluten-free.

The fact that there isn't a trace of gluten in our house doesn't define us or our dinner table. Yes, we are more conscious of what goes into our bodies, and we can't rely on wheaty staples for sustenance. Beyond that, we focus on cooking good food—food delicious enough to please the most committed omnivore. I like the challenge, and I am determined that our meals be damned good. Drool-worthy. Healthful. Delish.

Our meals are simple, delectable, seasonal, and fresh—they just happen to be gluten-free as well.

Food has always anchored my family. As a child, I loved everything about being in the kitchen with my mom while she made supper. A self-taught cook—with the help of all things Julia Child and a few Greek cookbooks from my paternal grandmother—Mom spent hours in her apron, creating warm, sumptuous meals for our family. As soon as I could, I cooked alongside her. Not only did I savor this closeness with my mom, but I also adored the meals we made together. Honey-oat bread hot from the oven slathered in butter, spanakopita bursting with spinach and feta and ricotta, spicy gumbos, creamy omelets, avocado sandwiches, silky chocolate mousse . . . I loved it all. Mom taught me that food was about enjoyment, that a meal should be relished and often cooked with friends. She also made sure I knew that food was about health and nourishment.

My parents were committed to organic, lovingly grown ingredients long before the word *locavore* was part of America's food lexicon. In 1970s Seattle, mom shopped at our local co-op, bought whole grains from bulk bins, and fed me raspberry kefir as an after-school snack. On weekends, we drove to the Pike Place Market to pick out the freshest king salmon and local honeys. Sugary cereal, white bread, and bologna were never options at our house. My parents even joined Seattle's P-Patch community garden, where we grew some of our own vegetables in the middle of the city. I have visceral memories of digging my tiny hands into the soil to discover potatoes hidden deep in the earth. A miracle, I thought.

When I was seven, Dad and I dressed in matching outfits for a Seattle Seahawks game. No, we weren't sporting royal blue jerseys emblazoned with the number of our favorite football player. We were head-to-toe orange—bright orange. In support of Washington state famers, Dad and I were dressed as carrots—a 6-foot-tall manly carrot and his little veggie sidekick. I'm sure we looked absurd, but Dad was an environmentalist; supporting farmers was an essential cause for him, and I was game.

After my parents divorced, we headed south. My dad moved to San Antonio, where he could finally warm his Greek skin in the Texas sun. Mom, my new stepdad, our three cats, one large U-Haul, and I headed for the foothills of the Sierra Nevadas. We were California bound. We settled in Nevada City, a tiny historic gold-rush town full of hippies, aggies, and Bay Area expat intellectuals. Mom bought five acres, and she and my stepdad got to work planting a huge organic garden. For years, they cleared the land, planted trees, tended the soil, and cultivated all kinds of gorgeous fruits and vegetables. While I loved eating the lusciousness the garden produced, I was too busy tending to my asymmetrical haircut and punk rock friends to be bothered with the garden or getting dirt under my nails. Mom picked me up from middle school in a dusty pickup truck wearing dirty overalls and a wide-brimmed straw hat. I was completely embarrassed. Why couldn't she perm her hair, wear tennis clothes, be normal, like the other moms?

Now, when I think back to my mom in those days, I see how beautiful she really was: her shoulders tanned from all the hard work she was doing in our garden, her face glowing from being outside, breathing deeply, and doing the truly satisfying work of growing food.

We found ourselves in Berkeley in the mid-'80s. I was in high school now, had a baby brother, my mom and stepdad were divorced, and we no longer had a veggie garden. Being a single parent with two kids, Mom had lost much of her passion for cooking elaborate dinners, so she and I worked together most nights to put a simple, nourishing meal on the table. Out of necessity, I learned how to cook and reveled in finding my own way in the kitchen. I began experimenting with ingredients and became adept at whipping up omelets, roasting salmon, putting together a lush salad—and making a quick, healthful, and tasty supper. But we also ate out a lot. Living in the food mecca that is Berkeley, we got to try a taste of everything. We scarfed Thai, sushi, salads from the local French deli, olallieberry pies, burritos galore, lattes, artisanal breads, Chicago-style pizzas. You name it. And when we splurged, Mom would take me to Greens, Fourth Street Grill, Zuni, or Chez Panisse.

Eating at these iconic Bay Area restaurants as a teenager rocked my world. We were never a family who craved "fancy" food per se. We had always been willing to drive hours to find the best barbecue joint, which I enjoyed just as much as lobster tail at the toniest restaurant. But this was something different. The food at these restaurants wasn't exactly fancy, yet it was powerful in a new way. The freshness, the flavor combinations, the homey perfection moved me deeply.

After living in Manhattan during my college years, I headed back to Berkeley. While I loved New York—the fashion, art, and energy of the city—I couldn't resist the Berkeley lifestyle. My now-husband, Paul, and I settled into a little cottage and nested. We gardened, cooked, and ate together. Paul and I embraced the food culture I'd fallen in love with while growing up.

....

Six years ago, I was diagnosed with celiac disease, an autoimmune disease that causes havoc and damage to the gut, and just months later our two young kids were diagnosed with gluten intolerance. I was devastated. What could we eat? How could I heal myself and feed a family? I felt deep loss and worried that a lifelong pleasure in adventurous eating had come to an end. Our social lives, which had always revolved around food, became fraught and complicated. Travel seemed impossible.

My diagnosis left me feeling isolated and alone—a pariah in a community of serious food lovers. To my dismay, I'd become one of those high-maintenance eaters who has long, tedious conversations about my special needs with every waiter, or with each dear friend simply wanting to have us over for a family supper. This was not me. I'd always prided myself on not being picky—even as a kid I ate everything with great enthusiasm. For me, food had always been a deep source of happiness and pleasure, but an aching belly and astute doctors told me that carefree eating was no longer possible.

I longed for the joy and ease I'd always found in the kitchen.

At first, I bought and ate all the packaged "gluten-free" foods I could find, but I quickly realized how empty they all tasted. Slowly, I made a mental shift around my new situation. After a year of healing and feeling forlorn, I started to look at our kitchen in a new way—not as a place of deprivation or limitation, but as one of abundance and possibility. I returned to cooking from scratch with natural, whole ingredients, to trusting my own cooking knowledge and instincts. I re-embraced our favorite comfort foods like scrambled eggs, meaty stews, and colorful salads and began to see that much of what we already loved to cook was actually safe for me to eat.

I stopped focusing on what we couldn't eat and embraced all that we could eat. Meats, veggies, fruit, fish, cheeses, eggs, olives, beans, rice, corn, endless herbs and spices: These wholesome and flavorful staples, the building blocks for most cuisines, are all naturally gluten-free.

Of course, we couldn't resist going well beyond basics. At the market, we bought broccoli but also snapped up rapini and romanesco. Cooking with black quinoa and red amaranth gave me a novel thrill. Pomegranate molasses, Pluots, and kumquats made me smile. Baking with buttery rich almond flour amazed me.

My celiac diagnosis had become an impetus for our kitchen habits to become richer and more varied as we welcomed the challenge of cooking abundantly delicious food without gluten. My "limitation" forced us to become more creative and expansive in our approach to food. Looking to nature's vast array of wondrous ingredients, we discovered a bounty of flavor and greater health.

We were even inspired to tear out our lawn and grow some of our own food.

Our backyard is now a tiny organic garden packed with vegetables, herbs, and seven little fruit trees, and we've involved our kids in every step of the process, from hauling compost (not their favorite task) to planting seedlings to harvesting, of course. It's not unusual for Otis and Lilah to wander outside and pick the vegetable they want to eat for supper.

We have never eaten so well.

In 2010 we went on a yearlong adventure: pulled the kids out of school, put our Berkeley lives in storage, and circumnavigated the globe. Traveling as a celiac with two gluten-intolerant kids was complicated and took a lot of planning ahead (and some serious snack packing.) We were happiest—and healthiest—when we really settled into a spot, shopped at local farmers' markets, and cooked for ourselves. We didn't have access to the endless ingredients we find at our Bay Area markets, yet we were able to make healthful meals that grounded us in place and gave us the deep comfort of feeding ourselves.

Our travels also introduced us to other cultures and their brilliant recipes, which were often naturally gluten-free. We not only lived on a Balinese rice field for six months, witnessing the entire harvest cycle just beyond our doorstep, but we also learned a lot about ancient varietals of rice and how to cook them in new ways. You'll find a smattering of travel-inspired recipes in this book, from Balinese black rice pudding to Australian almond tea cakes to pistachio kebabs in honor of our time in Istanbul.

Nothing felt like more of a welcome home than getting back to our Berkeley kitchen and garden. We cooked, planted, and nested once again. The kids returned to school feeling like they knew the world a little better and had a sense of what it tasted like. My boy, Otis, so unlike the garden-averse adolescent I was, now attends our neighborhood middle school, the home of Alice Waters's original Edible Schoolyard. He and his buddies can't wait for their time in the garden, where they look forward to getting their fingernails nice and dirty.

．．．

I'm an omnivore by nature and gluten-free by necessity. I am neither a professional chef nor a dietitian, but I am an unabashed home cook, voracious eater, and photographer. I'm also a mother of two with a deep commitment to a wholesome and varied diet for my family. Meals need to be easy, satisfying, and full of flavor and good health: realistic meals for people who love real food.

I see our kitchen as a place of possibility, a place of play, experimentation, and delight. I write this book hoping to bring a little extra joy to all of our kitchens, to inspire us to cook for ourselves and our families, and to remember that cooking need not be laborious, overly complicated, or full of wheat to be delicious.

Feeding those we love should be inclusive and expansive, and I strive for the food in these pages to be nourishing, fresh, and tasty enough to please everyone's bellies. So many of us feel better eating less wheat, and everyone seems to have at least one friend or loved one these days who's gluten-free. I hope this book will become a dog-eared guide for any food-loving home cook, a valuable resource full of gluten-free recipes that make everyone happy and excited to eat. I hope we can all find comfort at our dinner tables by embracing the delectable abundance that's ours for the taking.

an abundant
{GLUTEN-FREE}
pantry

Nourishing food is a pleasure we can have every day, gluten-free or not.

Our family lives by the simplest of all tenets, that a meal will only taste as good as the ingredients going into it. With little fuss, deliciousness can be had by using the best, freshest, most lovingly grown ingredients. Eat a perfectly ripe, organic tomato all by itself and it's really good. Add a sprinkling of salt and you have a treat. Splash on some good olive oil and roast the beauties at just the right temp . . . and you get magic.

I urge you to seek out the best ingredients—neither the fanciest nor the priciest, but just the ones in season, abundant, or maybe even growing in your own backyard. Then we can play with flavor and texture combinations and discover ways for preparing and savoring these natural delights.

When we look at ingredients as a kitchen's palette, the world of food is endlessly rich and varied. For those of us who cannot eat gluten, we remove only three items (wheat, barley, and rye) and still have thousands of tasty edibles to enjoy.

In our wheat-laden culture, it's dangerously easy to pick up another slice of pizza, eat a quick sandwich, nibble on a bagel, or snack on crackers. Removing gluten from our kitchens makes it more difficult to fill our bellies with such empty bites—thank goodness. Without gluten, healthful whole foods such as fruits, nuts, alternative grains, cheeses, veggies, and eggs take on a more appealing and essential role than ever in our lives. Luckily, the world is crowded with a myriad of wonderful ingredients that happen to be naturally gluten-free.

In this book, I encourage you to use less predictable ingredients and to look at your kitchens with a sense of discovery. I don't want to send anyone on a wild goose chase, but I do want us all to open our eyes wide at the market, to have fun and play with new foods. My hope is that your kitchen and approach to cooking and eating will become more expansive, and in turn more healthful.

That said, I would hate for you to feel beholden to a specific ingredient or rigid recipe. Instead, I hope you'll scribble notes in the margins of this book. Splatter olive oil, butter, berries, and wine on the pages. I hope you will take these recipes and make them your own.

a few tips for my gluten-free friends . . .

COOK AT HOME. It's the easiest, most healthful, and safest way to be gluten-free. Having a well-stocked pantry of quality basics allows you to make count-less recipes without much fuss. Let the larder work as the foundation of your healthful working kitchen while a seasonal flow of fruits and veggies lends depth, richness, and variety to your family table.

When you head to the market, be ready to CHECK YOUR LABELS. Become an expert on what you can eat and what you can't. (Even my gluten-intolerant kids are pros at reading labels. Before my daughter was old enough to read her-self, she would ask an adult or teacher to read aloud the ingredient list before she would dig in.) This vigilance sounds daunting at first, but then it just becomes part of life. Truthfully, we should all take more time to be aware of what we're putting into our bodies.

EAT WHOLE FOODS as often as possible. Look for foods that are simple, pure, and honest. Try to avoid buying products that are heavily processed, list-ing unidentifiable and unappetizing scientific names. Remember Michael Pollan and his brilliantly simple food rule: Don't eat anything with more than five ingredients or ingredients you can't pronounce. Pollan's motto is perfect for those of us who are gluten-free. Keep it simple, and eat real food.

DON'T FALL FOR TEMPTING "GLUTEN-FREE" MARKETING. If you are anything like I was when I first went gluten-free, I was thrilled to find so many "gluten-free" products available at the market. After spending months filling my shopping cart with all sorts of snazzy "gluten-free" packaged foods, I realized that I was feeding my family a lot of empty processed calories. (In fact, we were eating way more processed foods than we ever had before going gluten-free!) Thankfully, we're back to cooking primarily with whole foods, but I do make small exceptions and I buy a handful of gluten-free products to make our lives easier. I will share my favorite pastas, sandwich breads, and flour blends with you in the coming pages.

SHOP BULK BINS WITH CAUTION. I have long been a fan of the frugality and environmental benefits of buying from bulk bins at my local health food market. Sadly, if you have celiac disease or severe gluten sensitivity, this is an area of the store you will probably want to avoid. Cross contamination is an undeniable risk in bulk bins.

DON'T BE SHY. Advocate for yourself at your local grocery or health food store. Politely request specific ingredients and brands you want. I also encourage you to contact manufacturers or check their Web sites to make sure something is truly gluten-free. I sent countless e-mails to producers when I was first diagnosed with celiac disease to be certain that the products I bought were safe for me. We can all help in educating our own communities on how to live a healthful, wholesome, and abundant gluten-free life.

stocking the pantry

WHOLE GRAINS + SEEDS. Make friends and experiment with whole grains and seeds: millet, amaranth, buckwheat, quinoa, certified gluten-free oats, corn, and various rice varietals. Thankfully, Alter Eco and Bob's Red Mill have extensive lines of gluten-free grains and seeds. (I'm hopeful there will be even more organic options available soon.) Lotus Foods has a nice selection of organic

heirloom rice, ranging from black to red to brown. See my Grain + Seed chapter (page 149) for detailed recipes and ideas.

POLENTA + CORNMEAL. Bob's Red Mill is a great source for GF cornmeal, polenta, and masa harina.

CORN TORTILLAS + CHIPS. Gluten-free folks, chips and tortillas are our friends, but check the labels. I have found that more and more corn tortillas have "wheat gluten" or "wheat flour" in the ingredients. You can always make your own tortillas (page 177) using gluten-free masa harina.

GLUTEN-FREE PASTA. Bionaturae's gluten-free pastas get our vote. The noodles don't get gummy like so many GF pastas, and they're organic. Bionaturae makes spaghetti, fusilli, penne, and elbow pastas.

FLOURS. Pamela's Gluten-Free Bread Mix is my favorite all-purpose blend. I use it for all my tarts and galettes. (Keep in mind that there is a hint of sweetness.) Many GF folks have taken to mixing their own flours, and I applaud that, though I find that the ease of this store-bought blend works for our family. Pamela's pancake mix is also really good.

Sorghum and white rice flours are versatile and relatively flavor neutral, which makes them good for thickening gravy, dredging meat, and other similar uses.

Millet, oat, buckwheat, brown rice, and quinoa flours are all flavorful in their own distinct ways. See these grains and flours put to good use in my Grain + Seed chapter (page 149).

Nut flours are a gift to any kitchen. Ground nuts are not an inexpensive option, but the resulting creations are rich and nutritious. See my Nut chapter (page 189) for recipes.

GLUTEN-FREE BREADS. Canyon Bakehouse seven-grain bread is my favorite sliced sandwich bread.

Udi's millet-chia bread and whole grain bread are both good all-around sandwich breads.

Food for Life rice-millet bread is a tasty, dense, cake-like bread.

Mariposa Bakery has an incredible range of artisanal breads.

GLUTEN-FREE BEER. There is a growing list of GF beers on the market. I particularly like Green's Belgian Beers and St. Peter's Sorghum Beer.

GOOD OLIVE OIL. Make sure to buy true extra-virgin olive oil. You may want to consider buying a lighter, less expensive oil for cooking and a fruitier, more expensive oil for finishing and salad dressings. There is so much variety in the market that I encourage you to taste many oils and choose your favorite.

ASSORTED COOKING OILS. I fell in love with coconut oil when we lived in Bali. It's great for roasting veggies, cooking up stir-fries, and baking. You can also use coconut oil at higher heats than olive oil. Canola works well in combination with olive oil when making mayo at home. A splash of toasted sesame oil gives great flavor to stir-fries and Asian-inspired dishes.

VINEGARS. I admit it—I mostly use balsamic vinegar for my dressings, as I like the sweet-tangy combo. I also use a lot of apple cider vinegar. Champagne, red wine, white wine, and sherry vinegars also live in our cupboard, but honestly, I rarely use them. I occasionally splurge on saba for a special treat (see more about saba on page 92). {GF folks, be sure to avoid malt vinegar.}

DJION MUSTARD. I always buy a basic Dijon for my salad dressings, sandwiches, and other basic uses. See page 267 for my favorite simple dressing recipe.

TAMARI SAUCE. Soy sauce is one of those sneaky ingredients that contains wheat and must be avoided. Buy gluten-free tamari sauce as a substitute—it's delish!

EGGS. Not only are eggs wonderful as the star of a meal—often making meat unnecessary—but they are also amazingly helpful as a binder and moistener in gluten-free baking. Our favorite eggs come from the farmers' market, butcher shop, or occasionally our neighbor's coop.

MILK, CREAM, AND BUTTER. Organic is a must for us.

PARMESAN. This miracle cheese adds both salt and acid to any dish. Shave Parm onto eggs, into a soup, and onto salads or pastas. Save your rinds to add to soups for flavoring. It's said that the aging process of true Parmesan makes it easier to digest than other cheeses.

FETA + FRESH GOAT CHEESE. I use these two cheeses as flavor accents, especially to add a little protein and creaminess to vegetarian dishes.

YOGURT. I'm a huge fan of Greek strained yogurt, and now it's possible to buy organic (thank you, Straus Family Creamery). For those who cannot tolerate cow's milk, Bellwether Farms makes amazing sheep's milk yogurt.

DAIRY ALTERNATIVES. Almond and coconut milks are great options for folks who can't tolerate dairy. Luna and Larry's Coconut Bliss is the ultimate creamy frozen treat for GF folks who can't eat ice cream made with milk.

SWEETENERS. We try to use as little refined white sugar in our house as possible, though we are not dogmatic about it. I like to experiment with various natural sweeteners, as I enjoy the range of flavors and believe that variety is a good hedge on the health front. Honey, molasses, turbinado sugar, maple syrup, maple sugar, date sugar, coconut sugar, and light agave nectar are all ingredients we use to make sweet treats.

DRIED BEANS. I have a cupboard full of dried beans—everything from cannellini to Midnight Black to tiny flageolet. Rancho Gordo's heirloom varietals are my favorite. Every time I see a new type of bean at the market, I try it, and I am never disappointed. {GF folks: Be sure to give your beans a thorough rinse before cooking.}

JARRED TOMATOES. Tomatoes are one of the few seasonal goodies we cannot live without all winter long. We freeze homemade Candied Tomatoes (page 50) and buy jars of organic crushed or pureed tomatoes to add to soups, stews, and sauces.

GARLIC, ONIONS, AND SHALLOTS. We always have these flavorful friends on hand.

LEMONS. I couldn't live without lemons. A squeeze of citrus can brighten up most meat, fish, veggies, and grains. Before adding more salt to a dish, try adding lemon juice. And you can always use lemon juice in place of vinegar as the acid in your salad dressing. I'm partial to Meyer lemons, as I enjoy how perfectly their natural sweetness tempers the bitter notes.

FRESH HERBS. Homegrown herbs can transform your cooking. If you can spare the yard or some sunny window space, grow some herbs. They make everything better!

DRIED HERBS. We always have dried bay leaves, fennel seeds, and oregano ready to use.

SPICES. Look for the "gluten-free" label on all spices. Or contact the manufacturer. We buy Spicely Organic Spices.

SALTS. There is so much fun to be had with salt! My favorite salt is Maldon Sea Salt Flakes, which are pure heaven. I have also grown fond of using smoked salt, especially in my beans. Artisan Salt Company's Salish (alder-smoked fine salt) is fantastic. I like using pink Himalayan salt, gray salt, fleur de sel, and Balinese sea salt. Diamond Crystal kosher is our basic bulk salt. My overarching advice for salt use in your kitchen is to taste taste taste. Get to know your salt and how "salty" it is. Having a deep familiarity with the salt you use will make all the difference in your cooking.

FRESHLY GROUND BLACK PEPPER. There is no comparison of the flavor of freshly ground black pepper next to the ashy, dusty pre-ground stuff. Investing in a little pepper mill is worthwhile.

OLIVES. Olives are one of nature's rich treats, which of course are gluten-free as well. They make a great snack or simple appetizer option.

NUTS + NUT BUTTERS. Raw and toasted nuts and nut butters are wonderfully gluten-free. See my Nut chapter (page 189) for recipes and ideas. Store nuts in the fridge to prolong freshness.

BROTHS. We've become so attached to the flavor of homebrewed chicken and veggie broths that it's hard to go back to the store-bought kind. If you'd like to make your own broth, see pages 90 and 148 for my easy recipes. Store broth in your freezer until you need it.

Not everyone has the time, energy, inclination, or space to plant a veggie garden, but most of us have a sunny windowsill where a little pot of fresh herbs can happily grow. If you don't already, I urge you to try growing just a few. Having access to fresh herbs transformed my cooking. Snipped parsley turns grilled meat into a feast. Torn basil leaves add an undeniable brightness to a simple salad or pasta dish. And a pot of tea made from fresh mint, lemon balm, or verbena leaves is deeply refreshing in its clean, pure flavor.

. . . and on edible blossoms

One of the greatest revelations for me in filling our small backyard with edibles was learning that when plants go to seed, it isn't a bad thing. As arugula, broccoli, fennel, kale, parsley, and onions bolt for the sun, they bloom with little flowers, which turn out to be one of the garden's great (and tastiest) gifts. I like to pick these little flowers and add them to my salads, grains, and pastas in much the way you would snip fresh herbs over a dish. All the delicate flowers taste of the plant from which they sprouted. Often we'll snip some blossoms and stick them into a mason jar with water, making a little edible flower bouquet for our kitchen table. We can then pluck a flower or two to nibble on whenever we please.

slurp

lemon rosemary cordial

Traveling throughout New Zealand and Australia, we saw (and drank!) many cordials. I couldn't resist the charming bottled sweetness and, I must say, a cordial turns out to be just as welcoming as the name suggests.

Mixed with sparkling water, the concentrated sweet, herby flavor of this lemon cordial makes a delightful natural sparkling lemonade. You can also add a splash of cordial as a mixer to make a tasty cocktail. Keep in mind that the cordial is an intensely sweet and concentrated syrup, so a little goes a long way.

The cordials we encountered while traveling were always clear liquid, but I prefer leaving the ingredients soaking in the syrup. When you mix up a drink using your cordial, be sure to include a few strips of the soaking lemon peel, adding both beauty and flavor. (The rosemary gets a bit tired after soaking, so I discard it and add a fresh rosemary sprig to my drinks.)

makes about 2 cups

4 large juicy lemons	1 cup sugar
5 cups water	3 sprigs fresh rosemary

Rinse and scrub the lemons under a stream of cool tap water. Cut off the lemon peels into long strips, avoiding as much pith as possible. Juice the lemons and set aside.

Heat 4 cups of the water in a small saucepan over high heat. When the water is boiling, turn the heat down to a simmer, add the lemon peels, and blanch them for 4 minutes. Use a slotted spoon to remove the blanched peels and set aside. Pour out the blanching water.

Refill the small saucepan with the remaining 1 cup water and add the sugar. Turn the heat up to high and stir regularly to dissolve the sugar. Once the sugar has dissolved, add the blanched lemon peels to the pot. Cover and reduce the heat; simmer for 5 minutes. Remove the pan from the heat and add the rosemary and lemon juice to the pot. Stir. Let the lemony syrup infuse with rosemary as the liquid cools for 10 minutes or so. Transfer your cordial to a pint-size lidded glass bottle or jar. Store in the fridge for up to 1 month.

A few simple serving suggestions:

Fill a glass with ice and pour in 6 ounces sparkling water and 3 to 5 tablespoons cordial (depending on your sweet tooth.) Squeeze in the juice from ½ lemon. Add a few soaked lemon peels and stir. Use a fresh sprig of rosemary for garnish.

A boozier option: Over ice, mix 1 ounce gin (or vodka) with 2 ounces tonic water and 2 teaspoons cordial. Add a few soaked lemon peels and a generous squeeze of fresh lemon juice. Use a fresh rosemary sprig for stirring and garnish.

Tip: If you're willing to share, a bottle of cordial makes a friendly gift.

masala chai latte

There's no need to spend a wad of cash at Starbucks for a cup of creamy chai. When I learned how to make chai from Sujatha Kekada, a talented young Ayurvedic doctor working in Bali, I was amazed at how easy this belly-warming drink is to make from scratch.

I hope you'll use this recipe as a template for making your own chai. Feel free to make an ultrarich latte by substituting milk for all the water, or use decaf tea, or go unsweetened, if that's what you prefer. Add a little more of this spice, a little less of that, until you've created your own custom blend.

Tip: To make peeling easier, use the side of a spoon to scrape the peel right off your ginger.

serves 2 to 4

3 cups water

1 tablespoon peeled and grated fresh ginger

6 cardamom pods, lightly crushed in a mortar and pestle

½ teaspoon ground cinnamon

2 pinches freshly grated nutmeg

6 star anise

8 black peppercorns

1½ cups milk (cow, soy, and almond milk are all good)

6 teaspoons loose or 6 tea bags Assam or Darjeeling tea

Sugar, as desired (I like to add a couple of tablespoons of coconut sugar to the spice mixture)

Cinnamon sticks and/or star anise (optional), for serving

Place the water, ginger, cardamom, ground cinnamon, nutmeg, star anise, and peppercorns in a medium saucepan over medium-high heat.

When the liquid comes to a boil, add the milk. Let everything return to a boil.

Add the tea, reduce the heat, and simmer for 1 to 2 minutes. Keep your eye on the chai as it simmers, because it can bubble over before you know it.

Pour the hot chai through a strainer into cups or latte bowls. Add sugar according to your taste. Add a cinnamon stick and/or a few pieces of star anise to each cup, if you like, and sip right away.

slurp

mixed-berry slushie

My kiddos are always begging for slushies or icies—anything frozen, sweet, and delicious. Commercial varieties are packed with chemical coloring and high-fructose corn syrup, and I just cannot justify feeding such dreck to my kids. When I suggested to Otis and Lilah that we make our own slushies at home, they jumped to help. Even the neighbor kids came by to join the party. Making your own slushies is quick and super easy, and it's hard to resist happy kids with berry-stained chins!

serves 4

2 cups mixed fresh or frozen berries, such as strawberries, raspberries, blueberries, blackberries, and/or boysenberries

½ cup water

2 tablespoons freshly squeezed lemon juice

⅓–½ cup light agave nectar

2–3 cups ice cubes

Puree the berries, water, lemon juice, and agave nectar in a standing blender. Strain to remove the seeds. Thoroughly chill the fruit blend in your fridge, or do a quick chill in the freezer.

Place the chilled puree back in the blender with the ice. Blend until you have a nice slushie consistency.

Pour and slurp right away.

Tip: You can freeze any extra berry puree into popsicles or ice cube trays for future use.

hippie smoothie

Every morning as my family hustles to get ready for school, we try to maintain sanity and calm, but often a real breakfast just isn't possible. I've never had much of an appetite first thing in the morning, and neither do my kiddos. Back in the 1970s, in order to feed a sleepy girl (with an even sleepier belly), Mom would make smoothies for me as a quick, healthful, and easy-to-go-down breakfast. And here I am doing the same for my family.

This recipe is endlessly flexible and adaptable to seasonal availability and personal preferences. If you really want to up the hippie factor, toss in some chia or flax seeds, or even a scoop of nut butter.

I think we all deserve a forgiving breakfast recipe, don't you?

serves 2

1 cup chopped fresh fruit, such as strawberries, raspberries, nectarines, pears, or anything fresh, seasonal, and ripe

½ cup frozen fruit (berries and sliced peaches are my favorite)

1 banana

½ cup plain Greek yogurt (for those of you who cannot tolerate cow's milk, try sheep's milk yogurt)

Just enough orange juice to blend

Place the fresh and frozen fruit, banana, yogurt, and orange juice in a standing blender. Give it a whirl for 1 minute.

Serve right away, or pour your smoothie into lidded mason jars for breakfast to go.

peach and rose water lassi with crushed pistachios

If I see mango lassi on a menu when traveling through warmer climes, I cannot resist. The creamy sweetness is so refreshing! Living in a less-than-tropical spot here in Northern California, without a mango tree in sight, makes peaches a more accessible (and totally delicious) option for us when making lassis at home.

The silky flesh of a peach and the light perfume of rose water are so good together, and that salty crunch of pistachios gets me every time. This lassi makes a satisfying afternoon snack or a good companion to any spicy meal.

serves 2

1 cup fresh or frozen peaches, cut into chunks (1 large or 2 small peaches)

½ cup plain yogurt (use Greek yogurt for a thick lassi)

2 tablespoons milk

½–1 teaspoon rose water

2–3 tablespoons honey

Pinch of Maldon sea salt or any good sea salt

4 ice cubes

2 tablespoons coarsely chopped roasted salted pistachios

In a standing blender, combine the peaches, yogurt, milk, rose water, honey, and salt. Blend until everything is smooth and silky, then taste for sweetness. Add additional honey if you'd like it (especially if you're not using a sweet ripe peach) and even a little extra splash of rose water, if it pleases you.

Finally, add the ice cubes. Blend again, and serve topped with the pistachios.

ruby red grapefruit fizz

While we avoid the nastiness of sugar-filled sodas at our house, we still like to indulge in a sweet, fizzy drink every once in a while. Grapefruit juice, bubbles, and a hint of herby thyme are so fresh and tasty together. Plus, I appreciate the flexibility of a drink that stands on its own as deeply refreshing but that can also be transformed into a cocktail with very little effort. It's helpful to have such an easy crowd-pleaser in your hosting arsenal.

Tip: If you are not a fan of citrus pulp, feel free to strain some, or all, of it before making your fizz.

serves 4 to 6

2 cups freshly squeezed grapefruit juice (ruby red is my favorite, but any sweet, flavorful grapefruit will do)

2 cups chilled sparkling water

2–4 tablespoons light agave nectar

Plenty of ice cubes

4–6 sprigs fresh thyme

Splash or two of tequila in each glass (optional)

Place the juice, water, agave nectar, and ice cubes in a large jar with a lid. Shake a few times until everything is combined and the bubbles are dancing. Taste for sweetness and add more agave, as desired.

Pour the fizz over more ice cubes into individual glasses. Top each with a sprig of thyme. Add some good tequila, if you so desire.

cucumber gimlet

I vividly remember my first sip of a classic gimlet when I was in college in New York decades ago. I fell in love right then and there with the intense pucker of Rose's lime juice. After making my own version of lime syrup with fresh citrus, I knew I wanted to combine it with the crisp, fresh taste of cucumber. I'm so glad I did. Cucumber and lime are delicious together, and the vibrant skins of the cucumber give an almost otherworldly color to the drink.

If you can find them, use Persian cucumbers. Their delicate peels and lack of big seeds make them especially well suited to this cocktail.

Before juicing, roll limes against the countertop with the heel of your hand. It makes the whole process much easier.

serves 4 or 5

2 or 3 Persian cucumbers or 1 regular
  cucumber, seeded
½ cup freshly squeezed lime juice
½ cup water
½ cup light agave nectar

Your favorite gin (Hendrick's,
  with its flowery, botanical flavor,
  is my pick)
Ice cubes

Coarsely chop enough cucumber to get ½ cup. Slice the remaining cucumbers into thin rounds for garnish.

In a standing blender or food processor, thoroughly puree the lime juice, water, agave nectar, and chopped cucumber. Strain the pulp through a fine-mesh strainer.

For each drink, mix 2 ounces (¼ cup) booze with 2 ounces (¼ cup) cucumber lime syrup. Add ice cubes and cucumber rounds for garnish. Yum!

fresh garden tea

I've lived in Berkeley for 25 years, and Chez Panisse has played an influential and nostalgic role in my life. I remember eating downstairs with my mom for my 16th birthday and tasting soft-shell crabs for the first time. Paul and I have gone to the café for countless anniversaries and birthdays. Occasionally, Mom takes all four of us for a meal and Otis and Lilah feast like royalty, made to feel totally at home by the perennially warm staff. Anytime we have a reason to celebrate, we go to Chez Panisse if we can.

At the end of every meal, one can sip coffee or an aperitif, yet I most enjoy the tisanes, simple herbal infusions. For nearly 20 years we have brewed our own tisanes at home as well. We snip lemon verbena, mint, fennel fronds, lemon thyme, raspberry leaves, and/or lemon balm from the backyard, tuck them into a glass jar, and pour hot water over the top. Simple, fresh, and just right. Thank you, Chez Panisse.

To make your own brew, nestle a handful of herb sprigs into any glass jar and pour hot water over the herbs. Let the tisane steep for a few minutes before serving.

The infusion is delicious hot, or it can be chilled for a very delicate iced tea.

watermelon punch with fresh lime and mint

I can't think of a better way to spend a hot August afternoon than gnawing on slabs of ripe watermelon, spitting the seeds from the back stoop, and letting the sticky juices run free. This punch spiffs things up a bit while still reveling in the celebratory vibe of late summer. Inspired by watermelon *agua frescas* and mojitos, this vibrant punch is playful enough to serve at a kid's birthday or family picnic, or you can always spike the bowl with a bit of light rum and have yourself a summery cocktail.

Tip: Chill the simple syrup and watermelon puree for a few hours before you want to serve the punch. If time doesn't allow for pre-chilling, just add plenty of ice to your punch, and you'll be good to go.

....

serves 6

½ cup plus 2 teaspoons sugar

½ cup water

1 medium watermelon

2 or 3 large juicy limes

⅓ cup loosely packed fresh mint leaves

Light rum (optional), for serving

First, make your simple syrup: Combine ½ cup of the sugar and the water in a saucepan. Heat over medium heat until the sugar has dissolved. Let cool.

Cut off the watermelon rind and remove the seeds, if there are any. Fill a standing blender with watermelon chunks. Using your fingers or a wooden spoon, push down the watermelon until it releases a bunch of juice—this released liquid will help make blending easier. Blend thoroughly. Puree another batch of melon if you need to. After pureeing, you should have about 4 cups watermelon juice. You can strain the watermelon pulp at this point, but I really prefer the thicker texture with the pulp left in. Chill the puree in the fridge for a couple of hours.

Juice the limes until you have ¼ to ⅓ cup of juice. Coarsely chop the mint leaves. Crush the mint with the remaining 2 teaspoons of sugar using a mortar and pestle, if you have one. Otherwise use a wooden spoon in a bowl to pulverize the mint and sugar. When you're done, you will have a well-integrated mint-sugar paste. Stir the paste into the lime juice.

Mix the pureed watermelon with the lime-mint-sugar mixture. Add 2 to 3 tablespoons of the simple syrup. Taste for sweetness. How much simple syrup you need will depend on the natural sugar content of your watermelon and your own personal preference for sweetness. (Leftover simple syrup can be refrigerated and put to other uses in cocktails, or to sweeten your iced coffee or tea.)

Served the punch chilled. Give it a good stir before serving to integrate the ingredients. If you want to transform this punch into a cocktail, I suggest adding 2 tablespoons rum to each cup of punch.

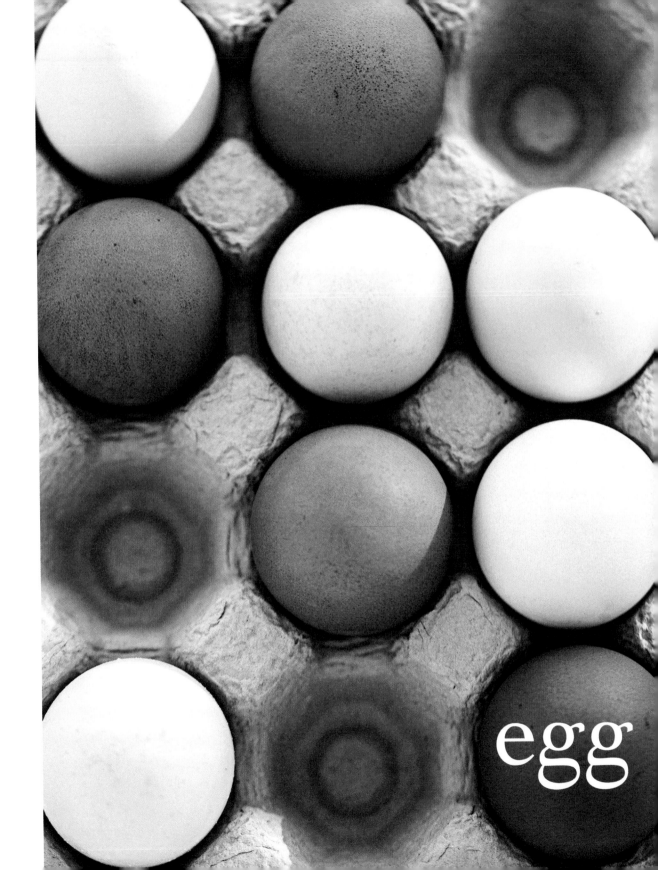

egg

spring omelets with asparagus and green garlic

Once you learn to make omelets, they become like a trusted friend—you know you can rely on them for warmth and comfort. While this particular recipe revels in the fertility of spring, we cook omelets year-round, especially for a late breakfast or cozy lunch.

Omelets can be stuffed with all sorts of goodies: goat cheese and freshly chopped herbs, bacon and spinach, wild mushrooms and Gruyère, crab and Parmesan, and so on. Once you feel comfortable making omelets, you'll find endless ingredients to experiment with in your own kitchen.

There is much debate about omelet-making techniques, yet I feel deeply grounded in this method. My mom taught me to make omelets this way when I was a teenager, and I've found solace in them ever since.

serves 2

6 to 8 ounces fresh asparagus spears, rough ends trimmed

1 teaspoon olive oil

2 tablespoons chopped green garlic, scallion, or leek

Sea salt

¼ cup grated Parmesan or Piave

2 teaspoons chopped fresh herbs, such as chervil, tarragon, and/or flat-leaf parsley

4–6 eggs

Freshly ground black pepper

2 teaspoons unsalted butter

First, blanch your asparagus until just tender. Cut the cooked spears into ¼" angled slices.

Heat the olive oil in a small skillet over medium-low heat. Add the green garlic to the oil. Cook for a minute or two, until the garlic is tender and aromatic. Add the chopped asparagus to the pan, stir to coat, add a pinch of salt, and cook for 1 minute. Transfer the asparagus and green garlic to a small bowl or plate, and set it next to your stove.

Start to warm your omelet pan over medium or medium-high heat. (I'm not a fan of nonstick pans, as their dubious toxic coating tends to peel, so we use a small, well-seasoned cast-iron pan for making omelets, and it works great. A little cast-iron or black steel pan is worth its weight in gold!)

Place the cheese and herbs in separate small bowls and set them near the stove.

In another bowl, thoroughly whisk 2 or 3 eggs (for 1 omelet). Add a pinch of salt, a few grinds from the pepper mill, and a small splash of tap water. Whisk to integrate.

When your pan is thoroughly preheated, adjust the heat to keep it hot, but shy of smoking. Plop in a pat (a teaspoon or so) of butter and tilt the pan to thoroughly coat all sides with the butter. (If the butter browns, wipe the pan with a paper towel, adjust your heat, and start again.)

When the butter has melted, pour in the eggs. Immediately tilt the pan to spread the eggs evenly over the bottom of the pan. After 15 seconds of cooking, or once big bubbles have formed, use a wooden spoon or spatula to pull back the eggs from the side of the pan, then tilt the pan, allowing runny egg to fill the void. Do this in four or five places, until you have a nice rumpled surface. Turn the heat to low and lay half of the asparagus mixture and half of the cheese onto the tender surface of your omelet. Cook the eggs a little more if you like your omelet well done. (I personally like mine soft, with a little runny middle.) Slide the omelet out onto a plate, folding it as it releases from the pan.

Top the omelet with 1 teaspoon of the herbs. Season with additional salt and freshly ground pepper, if you wish. Serve right away.

Quickly cook up the second omelet, and join your dining companion.

savory custards with wild nettles

A savory custard is a great tool to have in your eggy repertoire. Custards can be made a few hours before serving and eaten at room temp—a helpful flexibility when you're making brunch for friends. I discovered the basics for making savory custards in a wonderfully simple piece in *The New York Times* years ago and have been riffing on the theme ever since. While I am especially partial to these custards made with wild nettles, you can also use spinach as a more readily available substitute.

We happen to grow a little patch of nettles in our backyard garden, but you might also find them at the springtime farmers' markets. If you're bold enough to forage for wild nettles, beware of their sting. Stinging nettles are as vicious as their name suggests, which is too bad, because they're so irresistibly tasty.

serves 4

1¾ cups cream	1 tablespoon olive oil
¾ cup milk	Pinch plus ½ teaspoon sea salt
Couple sprigs fresh thyme	2 cloves garlic, finely chopped
3–4 cups fresh stinging nettle leaves (spinach is a good alternative)	3 eggs, at room temperature
	2 egg yolks, at room temperature
1 leek, thinly sliced, tender white end only	¾ cup grated Parmesan

Preheat the oven to 300°F. Butter four 4" ramekins.

Heat a kettle of water on the stove over high heat until hot but not boiling. (This water will be used for your custards' bath later.)

Place the cream and milk in a small saucepan along with the thyme sprigs. Turn the heat to medium. When the liquid starts to steam, remove the pan from the heat and let the thyme gently steep in the warm liquid while you prepare the rest of the custard filling.

When handling nettles, use gloves and tongs, and do not touch the raw plant directly or you will suffer that infamous sting. Wash the nettles and leave them wet. Carefully remove and discard the fibrous stems.

In a large skillet, cook the leek together with the oil and the pinch of salt.

Once the leek is tender, add the wet nettle leaves (or washed and trimmed spinach) and garlic and sauté until cooked through and tender. (Once the nettles are cooked, there is no more risk of sting, and you can handle them as you would spinach or any other green.)

Let the greens cool, then squeeze to wring out all the liquid. (Removing excess liquid is essential—otherwise you will end up with a watery custard.) Chop the greens, season with additional salt to taste, and scoop some into the bottom of each buttered ramekin. Place the ramekins, spacing them about 1" apart, in a large glass or ceramic baking dish (this dish will hold the custards' water bath).

In a large bowl, whisk the eggs, egg yolks, and the remaining ½ teaspoon salt until blended. Add the Parmesan.

Remove the thyme sprigs from the cream mixture. Slowly pour the mixture into the egg mixture, whisking continuously. Pour the liquid custard into each ramekin to cover the sautéed veggies.

Pour the hot (but not boiling) water from the kettle into the baking dish holding the ramekins. The water should surround the ramekins, reaching to 1" below the rims.

Bake the custards for about 35 minutes. To test for doneness, carefully tilt a ramekin to the side. If the center bulges but no liquid leaks out, they're done.

Remove the custards from the water bath and let them continue to set for 10 to 15 minutes after they've come out of the oven. Eat these delectable custards within a few hours of cooking, either warm or at room temperature.

poached eggs with lemony spinach + crispy hash browns

I've always been a sucker for diner food, especially when it comes to breakfast. I have fond memories of long family road trips when I was a child; every pit stop seemed to have the perfect toast, amazing hash browns, those cute little containers of grape jelly, and mini boxes of cereal. I liked it all.

But being gluten-free, eating at any old roadside diner has become impossible. As a result, I've been determined to master restaurant (and diner) classics in my own kitchen. Made at home, hash browns are gluten-free breakfast gold. Top those crispy potatoes with lemony spinach and poached eggs and I promise you'll feel anything but deprived.

For me, the ideal hash browns are cooked in a small skillet, a size just big enough to feed one person. You can make one order of hash browns at a time, keeping the first batch warm in the oven while cooking the second. Or you can go ahead and use a larger skillet to make enough hash browns to feed two.

serves 2

hash browns:

1 large russet potato

1 tablespoon unsalted butter

2 teaspoons olive oil

Flaky sea salt

spinach:

1½ cups steamed spinach

1 tablespoon olive oil

Zest and juice of 1 lemon

Sea salt

eggs:

4 eggs, at room temperature

1½ tablespoons white wine vinegar

for serving:

Flaky sea salt

Freshly ground black pepper

Preheat the oven to 250°F.

First, fill a medium saucepan halfway with water, and set it over medium heat. (This is your egg poaching water for later.)

Then make the hash browns: Peel the potato, and grate it using a standing cheese grater. You need about 1⅓ cups. Blot the grated potato with paper towels until you have absorbed as much of the excess liquid as possible. Dry potatoes are key to successful hash browns.

Heat a 6" to 7" skillet over medium heat. Put 1½ teaspoons of the butter together with 1 teaspoon of the olive oil into your hot, but not smoking, skillet. Scatter half the grated potatoes over the bubbling butter. (Try not to make the layer of potatoes too thick—nice lacy hash browns will help the potatoes cook through.) Cook the potatoes for 3 to 4 minutes, until you see browning and crisping throughout the lace of your potatoes. Flip and cook the other side until it's crispy golden brown, 3 to 4 minutes. (Don't worry if the hash browns fall apart as you flip, because they are forgiving and look beautiful when loose and messy.) Sprinkle the finished hash browns with sea salt, transfer to an ovenproof plate, and keep warm in the oven while you go ahead and make your next batch of hash browns. When you're done cooking both batches of hash browns, keep them in the warm oven while you poach the eggs.

Now it's egg-poaching time: Crack each egg into an individual small bowl or ramekin. Add the vinegar to the poaching water. When the water is hot but just below simmering, gently pour each egg into the water. (I suggest poaching in 2 batches.) Let the eggs poach for 2 to 3 minutes, until the whites have set and the yolks are still soft and runny. Use a slotted spoon to transfer the poached eggs to a plate lined with paper towels to soak up excess cooking water. (If you are a perfectionist, feel free to use kitchen scissors to trim the funky edges of the egg whites.) Poach the remaining eggs in this fashion. Cooked eggs can rest for a few minutes on the paper towel while you work. (If you are doing more than 2 batches of eggs, keep the cooked eggs warm in a bowl of warm water.)

The spinach: Just before serving, toss the steamed spinach with the oil, lemon juice, lemon zest, and salt to taste.

Plating time: Place half of the cooked hash browns onto each plate, scatter on some lemony spinach, and top with 2 poached eggs. Sprinkle with salt and pepper to taste. When the runny egg yolk mingles with the crispy potatoes and spinach, I'm in breakfast heaven, and I hope you will be too.

Tip: These poached eggs are amazing with the addition of a little scoop of Tarragon Pesto (page 97).

a breakfast salad with soft-boiled eggs, arugula, and toast

I have belly-warming memories of my mom making soft-boiled eggs for breakfast. She'd tear buttered toast into bite-size bits and toss them into a bowl, add the soft-cooked eggs, then mix the whole thing together. For me, it was a taste of morning comfort.

A nourishing breakfast is something I strive for with my own family. A few years ago, I remembered my love of soft-boiled eggs and began making them for my gang. Because I like to add greens to just about everything, I started throwing handfuls of arugula into my breakfast bowl. One morning as I happily ate my breakfast, my friend Abby remarked, "Hey, that's a salad."

Salad for breakfast? Yes, please.

serves 1

1 or 2 eggs

1 or 2 slices of your favorite bread for toasting {GF folks: see page xxii in "Stocking the Pantry" for suggestions}

Unsalted butter

Handful of arugula leaves

Sea salt

Freshly ground black pepper

Bring the eggs to room temperature by submerging them in a bowl of really warm (but not boiling hot) tap water. Fill a small saucepan with 3" to 4" water. Cover the pan with a lid and set over high heat.

Pop the bread into the toaster.

When the water is boiling, gently lower the eggs into the saucepan, and set your timer for 5 minutes 15 seconds. Adjust the heat to maintain a nice simmer. While the eggs are cooking, dump out the bowl of water you used to warm your uncooked eggs. Refill the bowl with cold water and a few ice cubes. When the timer goes off, quickly remove the eggs from the pot (using a slotted spoon is easiest) and immediately place the cooked eggs in the ice water bath while you finish prepping the rest of your goodies. The eggs can rest here for a minute or so, until they are cool enough to handle.

When your toast is ready, butter it and tear it into pieces. Nestle buttery toast bits in a small bowl. Scatter arugula leaves over the toast. Gently remove the eggs from their shells and scoop onto the bed of arugula and toast. Break the eggs in half and sprinkle everything with good sea salt and some freshly ground pepper.

egg in a hole

Sadly, I didn't discover this childhood classic until I was already in my twenties. When I was growing up, my mom made killer omelets and luscious soft-boiled and poached eggs, but this dish wasn't part of my family's repertoire. Paul, on the other hand, grew up with his mom making eggs this way. When he introduced this recipe to me, I was blown away by the clever simplicity. I may be well beyond childhood, but I feel like a gleeful kid every time we have Egg in a Hole for breakfast.

Paul's favorite thing about this dish is the circle of toast, which is cut away from the bread's center to make room for the egg and then gets panfried with plenty of butter. The little breakfast crouton begs to mop up the last drops of runny yolk.

....

serves 2

4 slices of your favorite sliced bread
    {GF folks: see page xxii in
    "Stocking the Pantry" for
    suggestions}

Unsalted butter

4 eggs

Sea salt

Freshly ground black pepper

Preheat a 9" skillet over medium heat.

In the meantime, place the bread slices on a cutting board. Get out a round cookie cutter to cut a circular hole in the center of each slice of bread. (We use a small juice glass with a 2" diameter lip. Turn the glass rim side down, place it over the center of a bread slice, and press down to cut a round hole out of each slice.)

When your pan is hot, melt a generous pat of butter (about a teaspoon). Place 2 slices of bread and 2 cutout rounds into the bubbling butter. Crack 1 egg into the empty center of each slice of bread. Let the eggs cook nestled in their little holes for a minute or two, until the undersides of the eggs and toast look cooked. Flip everybody over, add a tiny bit more butter to the pan, and briefly cook other sides. Don't overcook if you like a runny yolk, as I do. I use my fingers to press the egg whites to see if they're ready. If the whites are cooked and the yolks are still tender, you're done. Use a spatula to slide the eggs and toast onto a plate. Season with salt and pepper and serve right away.

Quickly cook up the second serving of Egg in a Hole while you chat with your breakfast cohort.

fried egg sandwich with pancetta and watercress

When I imagine biting into a bacon and egg sandwich, I swoon a little. Crisp salty bacon, runny golden egg yolk, and crunchy toast are made for each other.

I've made just a few adjustments to this diner classic. Watercress gives a peppery kick and adds just a hint of fresh brightness, while a flat round of well-crisped pancetta slides so nicely between the layers. Of course, the fried egg is its traditional happy self and seems perfectly willing to accommodate these flavorful friends.

Tip: Pancetta can be super salty, so I recommend using very thin slices. Or you can always use your favorite bacon as a substitute.

serves 1

1 round thinly sliced pancetta or
   1 slice bacon

1 slice of your favorite sandwich bread
   {GF folks: see page xxii in
   "Stocking the Pantry" for
   suggestions}

1 teaspoon unsalted butter

1 egg

Handful of watercress

Flaky sea salt (optional)

Freshly ground black pepper (optional)

Heat a skillet over medium heat. Cook the pancetta or bacon until crispy on both sides. Place the cooked pancetta on a piece of paper towel to absorb excess drippings. (If using bacon, tear it into 3 pieces after cooking it.)

Toast the bread until golden, and slather with the butter right away.

Wipe your skillet with a paper towel to soak up most of the pancetta drippings, but leave a glaze of drippings in which to cook your egg. Over medium heat, fry up your egg to your liking. I like my egg sunny side up, so after a few minutes of cooking, I turn down the heat and put a lid on my pan until the white has firmed up but the yolk is still nice and tender.

While the egg is frying, start to build your sandwich by layering the watercress and pancetta on the buttered toast so that you can slide the hot egg right into place. (You may or may not need any salt or pepper on the egg after it has cooked in the pancetta drippings—usually that's flavor enough.)

Eat immediately and don't worry if the yolk drips down your chin. In our house, that's the sign of a successful fried egg sandwich.

soft scramble with slab of aged cheddar + arugula

In 1999, Paul and I traveled to Sydney as a young married couple, and we fell in love with the gorgeous city. The warm weather was perfect, the turquoise bay sparkling, and the architecture full of Victorian charm. And we ate really well.

Our favorite spot was Bills of Darlinghurst, then a newish neighborhood haunt, before Bill Granger became the culinary superstar he is today. We couldn't resist eating breakfast at Bills every day for a week. I've never forgotten the simple scramble served with Cheddar and arugula. The combination of texture and flavor was just right: creamy custardy eggs, the salty purity of really good Cheddar, and fresh arugula. This recipe is a tribute to those sunny breakfasts in Sydney all those years ago.

For those of you who are used to scrambling eggs quickly, I urge you to give this low and slow method a try. You'll be rewarded with dreamy custardy eggs. This recipe can easily be adapted to feed a larger crowd or reduced to make a scramble for one.

serves 2

4 eggs

Splash of whole milk or heavy cream

Generous pinch of sea salt

1 tablespoon unsalted butter

1½ cups arugula

2 ounces aged Cheddar, sliced into thick slabs

Freshly ground black pepper

In a small bowl, thoroughly whisk the eggs, milk or cream, and salt.

Melt the butter in a small heavy-bottom saucepan over the lowest possible heat, then pour the eggs into the pan. Whisk the eggs regularly and let them cook low and slow. Be patient—it's worth the wait. You'll know the scramble is cooked when the eggs are soft and moist but no longer runny. Cooking time can range from 15 to 30 minutes, depending on how low your stove top's heat can go.

Transfer the eggs to 2 plates, along with a simple pile of arugula and a slab or two of Cheddar. Give the scramble a few grinds of fresh black pepper, and maybe another pinch of salt.

Tip: I like to serve this dish with a few slices of buttered millet toast. {See page xxii in "Stocking the Pantry" for suggestions.}

baked eggs on a bed of roasted cherry tomatoes

Juicy hot cherry tomatoes pop in your mouth. There's just a hint of basil for sweetness. When both mingle with creamy baked eggs, it's an amazing combination of texture and flavor that makes for very happy tastebuds.

These baked eggs are a hearty meal—even one egg, with its tomato companions, is surprisingly filling. You can easily increase or decrease the recipe depending on how many people you want to serve: Think 1 egg to ¾ cup tomatoes, and you're good to go.

Of course, you can serve these eggs for breakfast or brunch, but I'd eat them for dinner any day.

I highly recommend serving the eggs with a side of big buttery Croutons (page 263) or Polenta Fries (page 164) to soak up all the juicy goodness.

serves 4

3 cups sweet cherry tomatoes, halved

¼ cup grated Parmesan

2 tablespoons olive oil

2 tablespoons plus 1 teaspoon chopped fresh basil leaves

Flaky sea salt

Freshly ground black pepper

4 eggs, at room temperature

Preheat the oven to 400°F.

Scatter the tomato halves into a medium ceramic baking dish or cast-iron skillet. Bake the tomatoes in the hot oven for 12 minutes, then take the dish out. (If a lot of liquid has cooked out of the tomatoes, carefully pour off a little liquid now.) Top the tomatoes with the Parmesan, drizzle with the olive oil, and sprinkle on the 2 tablespoons basil and the salt and pepper. Then crack the eggs gently onto the bed of hot tomatoes. You want to keep the yolks intact, but don't worry when the egg whites spill down around the sides of the tomatoes.

Return the baking dish to the oven and bake for 8 to 10 minutes. You'll know you're done when the egg whites have set but the yolks are still soft. Sprinkle the cooked eggs with salt, freshly ground black pepper, and the remaining 1 teaspoon basil.

Serve right away in shallow bowls.

frittata packed with greens

A tender frittata is one of my favorite tasty vehicles for eating a ton of veggies and a good hit of eggy protein all in one delectable package. Since I'm mad for leafy greens of all sorts, I've come to make frittatas that are mostly vegetables, with just enough egg to hold everything together.

Remember, frittatas lend themselves to all sorts of additions. Try sautéed mushrooms, zucchini, asparagus, nettles, leeks . . . the possibilities and combinations are endless.

Tip: If you're using a hearty green like kale, steam it lightly before sautéing.

serves 4

4 cups tightly packed trimmed and chopped kale, chard, or mustard greens

4 cloves garlic, thinly sliced

2 tablespoons plus 1 teaspoon olive oil

Sea salt

6 eggs

Pinch of freshly grated nutmeg

¼ teaspoon red-pepper flakes

Freshly ground black pepper

¾ cup grated Gruyère (Parmesan and/or goat cheese also work well here)

Dollop of Pistachio Pesto (optional; page 195)

Sauté the greens and garlic with 2 tablespoons of the oil in a skillet for a few minutes, until the leaves are tender and the garlic is golden. Season with salt to taste.

While the greens and garlic are cooking, whisk the eggs, nutmeg, a generous pinch of salt, the red pepper, and black pepper together in a large bowl. Add the cooked greens and all but a handful of cheese to the bowl. Stir.

Turn on your broiler.

Place a 9" well-seasoned cast-iron or ovenproof skillet on the stove top over medium-high heat. Add the remaining 1 teaspoon oil to the pan and use a paper towel to rub it all around. Make sure the oil and pan are nice and hot but not smoking (a hot pan is key to the frittata not sticking). Then pour in the egg mixture and turn the heat down to medium-low. Sprinkle the last handful of cheese over the top.

Let the frittata cook on the stove top for 5 to 6 minutes, until the egg along the edges has set but the center is still loose. (With the help of a butter knife, the frittata should easily lift away from the sides of the pan.)

Pop the frittata under the broiler to finish cooking. Keep an eye on it: You want the eggs to be just cooked but not well done, so a minute or two of broiling is plenty. A moist frittata is what you're looking for.

Flip onto a plate. Flip again, so the pretty side is facing up. Sprinkle with a little salt and add some pistachio pesto, if you like.

veg

baby artichokes with plenty of lemon

To me, artichokes are the ultimate in edible blossoms. Looking at the thorny thistle, it's hard to imagine such a tender delicacy is hiding within its tough outer leaves.

I have early childhood memories of gleefully peeling back petals from big artichokes and dipping them into warm butter. We still eat artichokes this way at our house, but we've also added baby artichokes to our repertoire, and they are delish. My girl, Lilah, especially loves artichokes—when I cook them this way, she starts to pant and cheer with delight.

In the early spring, keep your eyes open at the farmers' market for the debut of baby artichokes. If you're lucky, you'll continue to find these edible flowers throughout the summer and even into fall.

Tips: A couple of things to keep in mind about baby artichokes: First, they are usually too young to have developed any choke at all; and second, trimming off outer leaves of the baby artichokes will reduce the size by more than half, but I think the tenderness and flavor make the sacrifice worthwhile.

serves 3 or 4 as a small side

16 baby artichokes (any variety will do)

Juice of 2½ lemons

2 tablespoons olive oil

Sea salt

¼ cup chopped fresh flat-leaf parsley

Zest of 1 lemon

A few salt-cured black olives, chopped (optional)

Peel off the outer leaves of your artichokes until you get to the tender, light green inner leaves. (You'll be surprised by how many layers you will have to remove before getting to these pale inner beauties. Just keep going.) As you prep the artichokes, submerge them in a bowl of cool water with the juice of ½ lemon, which will keep the tender, naked artichokes from oxidizing too much.

Use your paring knife to trim the rough outer layer off each stem and slice the pokey tops off the artichokes. (If the artichokes do have any chokes, remove and discard them now.) Next, use a sharp knife or a mandoline to slice

the artichokes as thinly as possible—don't worry if they fall apart. Return the slices to the lemon water.

Heat a large cast-iron skillet over medium heat. Add the olive oil to the pan. Cook the artichokes, shaking the handle of the pan regularly or stirring to help ensure even cooking.

After 15 to 20 minutes, when the artichokes are tender and cooked through, turn off the heat. Leave the artichokes in the hot pan, salt them generously, and drizzle with the remaining lemon juice. The lemon juice will sizzle and mingle with the olive oil in the hot pan. Top with the parsley and lemon zest and serve directly from the pan. Add some chopped olives to the dish, if that strikes your fancy.

massaged kale salad with dried cranberries, pistachios, and kumquats

At our house, we eat kale every which way and have devoted an entire bed of our backyard garden to growing these super greens. We toss leaves into soups, add them to frittatas, crisp them in the oven, and more often than not we simply steam up mounds of greens and drizzle on a little olive oil and nice sea salt.

In this recipe, kale steals the show in an entirely different way. Massaging the raw leaves breaks down the fibers until the hearty greens become tender, glistening, and luscious, like seaweed. It's hard to believe this texture transformation until you try it for yourself. The massaged kale really shines when you add some tasty cohorts to the mix: Crunchy pistachios and sweet dried cranberries, along with citrus and a hint of maple syrup, make for a kale lover's delight.

Tip: If you are new to kumquats, welcome to a real treat. With these little cuties, you want to eat the peel—that's where the sweetness lies. Slice them into thin rounds with skins on, pick out any seeds, and toss 'em into the salad. If you can't find kumquats, go ahead and use tangerine slices and an extra squeeze of lemon juice.

....

serves 6 to 8 (this salad easily feeds a crowd, but if you are the fiends for greens as we are, the recipe makes 4 generous servings)

⅓ cup extra-virgin olive oil

3 tablespoons freshly squeezed lemon juice

1 tablespoon maple syrup

¼–½ teaspoon sea salt

2 large bunches kale (8–9 packed cups), fully dried after washing

8–10 kumquats, thinly sliced into rounds (if you can't find kumquats, substitute 1 or 2 tangerines, peeled and sliced, plus an extra squeeze of lemon juice)

⅓ cup sweetened dried cranberries

⅓ cup chopped roasted salted pistachios

In a very large salad bowl, whisk the oil, lemon juice, maple syrup, and ¼ teaspoon of the sea salt.

Discard the tough ribs of your kale. Lay the leaves on top of each other, roll them up like a cigar, and chop widthwise into thin strips, a rough chiffonade. Add the leaves to the salad bowl, then use your hands to massage the dressing into the kale. After 3 to 5 minutes of massaging, the fibers will break down and the leaves will feel like silky seaweed. (If any tough rib pieces emerge during this process, toss them out. We only want the tender leaves.)

Toss the massaged kale with the kumquat slices, dried cranberries, and pistachios. Add additional salt and lemon juice to taste.

Tip: Leftovers keep surprisingly well—store overnight in a lidded container in the fridge.

candied tomatoes

There is nothing like the deep flavor of roasted tomatoes to combat the winter doldrums. You heard me right: I'm talking about tomatoes in winter. This recipe is all about taking advantage of summer produce at its peak and giving us access to summer delights well into the winter months.

If you are lucky enough to grow your own tomatoes, this is a perfect way to turn your bounty into an ingredient you can enjoy long after the summer sun has set. If you are like us and love tomatoes but don't grow them yourself, don't despair. When the days are hot and the time is right, go out and buy bags of your favorite local tomatoes. I hit the market in August and September, when our Northern California tomatoes are at their sweetest (and their prices are at their lowest), and I get to work candying dry-farmed Early Girls by the crateful. I toss them into freezer bags, and the juicy roasted tomatoes are ours to savor year-round.

Feel free to double or even quadruple this recipe. You won't be sorry when you have a stash of sweet roasted tomatoes waiting for you in the freezer. See Candied Tomatoes put to use in these recipes: Pork Ragù (page 133) and Cozy Winter Soup with Fennel Sausage, Leeks, White Beans, and Rapini (page 119).

makes about 1½ cups

4 pounds tomatoes (I'm partial to dry-farmed Early Girls—they may not look fancy, but the flavor is unbeatable)

2–4 tablespoons olive oil

Sea salt

1½ tablespoons sugar or 1 tablespoon light agave nectar

Preheat your oven to 250°F.

Slice small or medium tomatoes in half and spread them out, face up, over a large baking sheet. (If you are using huge heirloom tomatoes, cut them into large wedges.) Lightly drizzle the olive oil over the tops of the tomatoes. Sprinkle with salt. I like to sprinkle on a bit of sugar or drizzle on a bit of agave nectar to enhance the caramelization of the slow roast. Slide the baking sheet into the warm oven.

After 4 to 5 hours of roasting, your tomatoes will be ready. They will have shrunk in size significantly and the flavors will have concentrated. The tops will be caramelized, but the tomatoes will still be nice and juicy.

If you're like me, you'll need to go ahead and eat some roasted tomatoes right away—they are hard to resist. Maybe make yourself a bowl of roasted tomato pasta {see page xxii in "Stocking the Pantry" for GF pasta suggestions} with fresh basil, mozzarella, plenty of olive oil, and garlic. Or how about roasted tomato soup?

Tip: To save some Candied Tomatoes, fill a resealable plastic bag or two and store them in your freezer. When you pull them out in deep winter, you'll smile as you taste a bit of summer.

sunshine soup with heirloom tomatoes, mixed peppers, and basil

In high summer, when the sunny colors of tomatoes and peppers call to you at the market, you know it's time for Sunshine Soup. This vibrant pureed soup couldn't be much easier to make, and it's a family-friendly crowd-pleaser—something we all need in our bag of tricks.

This soup satisfies a variety of uses and audiences: Kids slurp it up and it's a great vegetarian option as well. Plus, it's a flexible canvas for all sorts of topping options. Croutons and pepitas are both great here, as are fresh basil and parsley. A dollop of crème fraîche is always nice as well. For those of you who like some spice, feel free to add chile oil or red-pepper flakes. This soup can be served warm, at room temp, or chilled. Easy, right?

Tip: To make your own pepitas, toast ¼ cup pumpkin seeds in ½ teaspoon of olive oil over medium-low heat until golden and crisp.

serves 4

soup:

7–8 cups mixed heirloom tomatoes cut into large wedges

2 large bell peppers or 8–10 smaller Gypsy peppers (mixed yellow, red, and orange), seeded and halved

½ cup loosely packed whole fresh basil leaves, plus more for garnish

⅓ cup extra-virgin olive oil

Sea salt

Pinch of freshly ground white pepper

toppings (optional):

¼ cup pepitas

Chopped fresh basil leaves

Dollop of crème fraîche (see page 266 for making your own)

Garlicky croutons (see page 263)

Chile oil or red-pepper flakes

Preheat the oven to 425°F.

For the soup: Place the tomatoes, peppers, and ½ cup basil leaves in a 13" x 9" ceramic or glass roasting dish. Pour the olive oil over the veggies and season with salt to taste. I use a teaspoon of salt myself. Give the goodies a toss

with your hands, if you are so inclined. I find that hands do a much better job than any spoon.

Roast the veggies for 30 to 40 minutes, until the tomatoes and peppers are tender, juicy, and just hinting at a char around the edges. Let everything cool to room temp.

Puree the vegetables thoroughly in a standing blender or food processor. (I use my standing blender and do the pureeing in a few batches.) Season with additional salt and some ground white pepper.

Serve with the pepitas, chopped basil, crème fraîche, and/or garlicky croutons, as it pleases you. Add chile oil or red-pepper flakes if you like it spicy.

old school caesar

I have a vague memory of going on a pilgrimage to Tijuana with my dad in the early 1980s. A Mexican border town renowned for all sorts of vice may seem like an odd place for a father to take his 10-year-old daughter on vacation. But in our family we have always traveled for the food.

Dad and I had a tradition of making Caesar salads together, and we needed to go to the source—we were going to Caesar's Restaurant in Tijuana to taste the original. I don't remember much about the meal, other than Dad spying on the tableside dressing action and taking mental notes. What I do know is that 30 years later, I still regularly make Caesars for my family and continue to hold a bit of pride and salad-making empowerment in that Dad and I tasted the real thing in TJ.

It's traditional, according to the daughter of Caesar's originator, to eat the romaine uncut. In our house we pick up the dressing-soaked leaves with our fingers, and it's messy good.

If you are making this salad for a dinner party, I suggest prepping the croutons and washing the lettuce ahead of time. (Store the croutons in an airtight container.) You can always serve the salad deconstructed: stack of leaves, pile of croutons, dressing in a bowl. Dip and go!

serves 4

croutons:

1½ cups bread torn into bite-size chunks (country-style bread or baguette works best for croutons) {GF folks: if you can't find gluten-free baguettes at your grocery, use your favorite white GF sandwich bread or even GF hamburger buns}

1 tablespoon olive oil

Pinch of sea salt

salad:

1 large head romaine lettuce or 4–6 heads Little Gem lettuce

1 clove garlic, peeled

Sea salt

1 or 2 good-quality anchovies

1 teaspoon Dijon mustard

1 egg yolk*

1 tablespoon fresh lemon juice

Splash of Worcestershire sauce

¼ cup extra-virgin olive oil

2 tablespoons finely grated Parmesan, plus more for serving

Freshly ground black pepper

Preheat the oven to 375°F.

For the croutons: Scatter the torn bread onto a baking sheet. Toss the bread with the olive oil and sea salt. Bake until golden brown, 8 to 14 minutes. Set the croutons aside and start making your salad.

Prep your lettuce: Remove and discard any funky or tough outer leaves, then wash and thoroughly dry the good ones. (I like to lay my clean lettuce leaves out on a big bath towel, wrap them up, and store the towel in the fridge while I prep the rest of the salad.) Chilled, super-dry leaves will let the dressing really cling to the greens come serving time.

Now the dressing: Using the tines of 2 forks, smash and shred the garlic clove and ¼ teaspoon sea salt against the bottom of a large wooden salad bowl. Next, add the anchovies, treating them the same way you did the garlic, using forks to shred them and integrate them into the garlic, making a thick paste. Whisk in the mustard. Add the egg yolk and continue to whisk everything with your forks. Next, whisk in the lemon juice and Worcestershire sauce. Now, slowly drizzle in the olive oil while continuously whisking to get a nice emulsified dressing. Finally, add the Parmesan and some freshly ground pepper to the dressing.

At this point, test your dressing by dipping a piece of lettuce into the bowl. You should taste that delightful combo of salty, tangy, creamy, and fresh. Add a little more salt or lemon juice as needed to get just the right flavor.

Toss the lettuce and croutons into the bowl—they will soak up any extra dressing at the bottom of the bowl (yum!). Serve the salad right away, sprinkled with additional Parm and pepper.

Eat raw eggs at your own discretion.

buttery peas with sautéed spring onions and fresh dill

Peas are one of spring's great gifts. Those elegant tendrils seem to sprout from the ground overnight, and the charming pods sing of fertility. The vibrant green of the little cuties evokes freshness, a symbol of all the brighter months to come.

Quick and easy veggie sides are a must in our house, and we like to simply prepare whatever happens to be in season. Even our pickier eaters (I won't name names) are game to try veggies that look recognizable as their natural selves, and that suits me fine. It pains me to interfere too much with the deliciousness of nature.

These are good with Succulent Lamb Chops (page 122) or Halibut Baked in Parchment (page 97).

serves 4 as a small side

2 small spring onions or 1 small shallot

1 tablespoon unsalted butter

2 cups shucked fresh peas (about 2 pounds in the pod)

1 tablespoon chopped fresh dill

Zest and juice of 1 small lemon

Sea salt

Fill a stockpot or large saucepan with water and bring to a boil.

Thinly slice the bulb ends of your small spring onions, making about a loose ¼ cup of slices. Also chop enough green leafy stem of the onions to fill 1 tablespoon, and save these greens for garnish.

Melt the butter in a small skillet over medium-low heat, add the sliced onions, and cook for 7 to 9 minutes, until tender and golden. Turn off the heat and let the cooked onions sit for a few minutes while you finish prepping the peas.

Blanch the peas in the boiling water for 4 to 6 minutes, until tender and vibrant green. (Time will vary depending on size and age of the peas.) Transfer to the pan and toss with the onions (and their cooking butter) over low heat until coated. Transfer to a serving dish. Add the dill, reserved onion greens, and lemon zest and juice and toss. Season generously with salt and additional lemon juice to taste. Serve right away.

zucchini ribbon "pasta"

Who says pasta can only be made from grains? Not me.

Zucchini lends itself to being sliced into beautiful, paper-thin, pasta-like ribbons. After a couple of minutes in a hot pan, these tender ribbons are ready to be tossed with all sorts of toppings. We usually eat zucchini pasta as a light side dish with a simple dousing of lemon juice, a hint of feta, and a smattering of fresh herbs, but the ribbons are also delicious with quickly seared cherry tomatoes, kernels of sweet corn, and chopped basil. Another perennial favorite is zucchini pasta graced with a few scoops of Pistachio Pesto (page 195).

serves 4 as a side

4 large or 6–8 small zucchini, ends
    trimmed

Olive oil

Sea salt

Zest and juice of 1 large or 2 small
    lemons

2 tablespoons cup crumbled feta

1 bunch fresh mint or basil, chopped

Using a mandoline or simple vegetable peeler, cut thin strips, or ribbons, of zucchini. Shave 2 or 3 strips off a side, and then rotate the zucchini and continue slicing. Then rotate again. Keep working your way around the zucchini until you get to the seedy middle. Discard the core.

Heat a tablespoon of olive oil in a large skillet over medium heat. When the oil is hot but not smoking, add a generous handful of ribbons to the pan. Toss to coat with olive oil. Add a pinch of sea salt. Cover the pan for a minute, allowing the zucchini to steam a bit. Uncover and continue to sauté the veg for another minute or so, until the zucchini is tender, bright, and just cooked through—al dente.

Set aside the cooked ribbons as you continue to sauté zucchini in batches until done. Add an additional splash of olive oil to the pan for each new batch. (Don't worry about the zucchini cooling down, because this dish can be served warm or even at room temp.) Finally, give your cooked zucchini a generous squeeze of lemon juice so the citrus can blend with the oil.

Heap zucchini ribbons onto individual plates. Sprinkle with the lemon zest, feta, and herbs. Add a little more sea salt if desired, though this usually isn't necessary with the salty feta and flavorful lemon juice.

veg

beet salad with mixed greens, walnuts, ricotta salata, and orange zest

I've always been a beet lover. Luckily, Paul regularly roasts beets throughout the colder months so that we have them ready to toss into salads with ease. I like to soak the roasted and peeled beets in the dressing so they can absorb the tangy vinegar and orange juice. The infused beets are wonderfully matched with the crunchy walnuts, fresh salad greens, salty ricotta, and earthy walnut oil.

Tip: If you are fortunate enough to get beets with the greens still attached, trim, wash, and sauté them the same day you get home from the market. You can treat them as you would spinach or chard, and they are such a treat.

. . . .

serves 4

3 large or 5 smaller beets

2 tablespoons red wine vinegar

2 tablespoons freshly squeezed
    orange juice

Flaky sea salt

½ cup raw walnut halves

¼ cup walnut oil or extra-virgin
    olive oil

6 handfuls mixed baby salad greens

Zest of 1 orange

2 ounces ricotta salata, crumbled

Preheat the oven to 400°F.

    Trim the beet greens to about 1". Leave the skins on the beets and place them in a baking dish. Splash ½ cup of water over the beets. Cover the baking dish with aluminum foil and roast the beets until tender. Small beets may need only 45 minutes, and large ones can take up to 1½ hours until they're fully cooked. To check for doneness, poke the beets with a sharp knife, which will easily penetrate a cooked beet. When the beets have cooled enough to handle, slide the skins off and slice into thin wedges. Turn the oven down to 350°F for toasting the walnuts.

    In a medium bowl, whisk together the vinegar, orange juice, and ¼ teaspoon salt. Add the sliced beets to the bowl. Toss to coat. Macerate the beets in the marinade for at least 30 minutes.

Toast the walnuts in the oven for 6 to 10 minutes, until golden. Chop coarsely. (Dehydrated Walnuts, page 208, are also delicious here.)

When you are ready to assemble your salad, pour the marinade out of the bowl holding the beets and into a large salad bowl. Whisk the oil into the marinade until you have a luscious salad dressing. Season with salt to taste.

Add the greens to the salad bowl. Toss to coat the leaves with dressing. Get out 4 small plates and scatter one-quarter of the dressed greens onto each plate. Top each salad with sliced beets, toasted walnuts, grated orange zest, and crumbled ricotta salata. Give another sprinkling of flaky salt and serve right away.

radishes with homemade herb butter and salt

A tray of perky radishes with a little ramekin of creamy homemade butter and sea salt: We have the French to thank for many culinary delights, and this simple appetizer is one of them. (Little tea sandwiches with thin rounds of spicy radish, herb butter, and salt are another tasty variation on this theme.)

Quality store-bought butter is of course fine with the radishes, but just-whipped butter made with organic cream and sprinkled with finishing salt . . . well, that's the good stuff, and it's not at all hard to make your own. How many times in my life have I kicked myself for over-whipping cream? Well, if you've experienced this same frustration, why not just keep going until you have homemade butter? It really is easy, and I'm guessing you'll be as happy as I am not to toss out the cream you bought.

....

serves 6 as an appetizer

1 cup heavy cream, at room
temperature
1½ teaspoons finely chopped fresh
tarragon or chervil

2 bunches fresh radishes (look for
radishes with healthy greens still
attached), trimmed
Any good salt, such as Maldon, pink
Himalayan, or gray sea salt

Using a handheld mixer and a large bowl, or a standing mixer with the whisk attachment, whip the cream on medium-high speed. Go way beyond whipped cream and keep beating. Occasionally use a spatula to scrape down the sides of the bowl. The cream will go through many phases, from fluffy whipped cream to a curdled mess. Don't despair—this is good. When the curdled creamy bits (the butter solids) turn yellow, firm up a bit, and separate from the liquid (buttermilk), stop mixing. Think of well-done scrambled eggs in a puddle of water. This will happen after 6 to 8 minutes of whipping.

Now it's time to get rid of the buttermilk. Pour the mixture through a mesh strainer, or a few layers of cheesecloth, and feel free to save the butter-milk for later use. Use your fingers to press down on the butter solids to squeeze out all remaining buttermilk—at this point you should be able to form a ball of butter. Be sure to rinse your butter by running it under very cold tap

water (or even ice water), which will help keep the butter from spoiling. Squeeze the butter one last time to make sure all excess liquid is gone.

Scoop the butter, along with the herbs, into a little jar or ramekin. Use a fork to blend.

I like to serve my radishes on a pretty plate, with a bowl of unsalted herb butter, and another dish of sea salt. Dip a radish into the butter, or spread a little butter on a radish with a knife, then sprinkle with salt just before taking a bite.

Tip: Whatever butter you don't eat with your radishes can be used to cook up an herby omelet, spread on your morning toast, or melt onto a piece of grilled fish or chicken for supper. Keep extra butter covered in the refrigerator and use within 5 days.

a wild salad

The notion of wild foods began to enter my consciousness just a few years ago. Of course, I have always enjoyed picking blackberries along the side of the road, and I do have fond memories of my dad teaching me to fish in chilly streams. Other than these small moments, I hadn't thought much of food that came from beyond the market, farm, or backyard garden.

Six years ago, I was walking near my mom's house in Bolinas with my boy, Otis, only 7 years old at the time. He pointed out a wild edible to me: "Mom. Mom, you've got to try this! It's delicious." He stuck a weed near my face and urged me to take a taste. Otis, who had recently learned of miner's lettuce on a school field trip, introduced the rest of us to a treat we now look forward to seeing every spring. Whenever we find a patch, we all love to pick and nibble on the raw, spinach-like leaves, and Otis suggested we make a salad with our wild treasure.

If you don't have miner's lettuce sprouting in your town, I'm certain there are other wild edibles nearby just waiting to be enjoyed—maybe wild plums, dandelions, stinging nettles, fiddlehead ferns, flowering nasturtium. . . . Needless to say, it's dangerous to go around nibbling on unknown plants, so do your research or take a guided foraging walk. Explore. If you're like me, you'll be awed by the bounty growing just down the way.

serves 4

4 handfuls miner's lettuce (If the lettuce is flowering, you can still eat it. The little blooms are so good!)

1 Meyer lemon or tangerine, quartered

Extra-virgin olive oil

Sea salt

The delicate leaves of miner's lettuce wilt quickly once dressed, so I wouldn't recommend dressing a big bowl of salad before setting it on the table. Instead, pass around small individual salad plates, each with a handful of just-picked leaves and a wedge of lemon. Then let everyone drizzle on a tiny bit of really nice olive oil, a squeeze of citrus, and a sprinkling of sea salt just before digging into the plate of tasty weeds.

parsnip crisps

These crisps inhabit a delicious world somewhere between shoestring french fries and sweet potato chips. Baking wisps of parsnip with coconut oil turns a less-than-healthy snack concept into an easy way to nibble on root veggies. Coconut oil brings out the natural nutty sweetness of the parsnips, and a hint of nutmeg gives each bite a little surprise.

The crisps make for a good snack food on their own, or they are delicious served with burgers, roasted chicken, or pork chops.

Quick to make and fun to eat: What more can we ask of a humble parsnip?

serves 4 to 6

1 pound parsnips (try to find small or medium parsnips)

2 tablespoons coconut oil, melted

Freshly grated nutmeg

Sea salt

Preheat the oven to 325°F.

Trim the ends off the parsnips. Peel and discard the outer layer of rough skin. Using a standard vegetable peeler, continue to peel long, narrow, irregular ribbons of parsnip. When you get to the tough core, discard it or save it for making veggie stock later. Place the parsnip strips in a large bowl and pour on the melted coconut oil. Toss to coat.

Scatter half the parsnip ribbons onto a large baking sheet. (I cook my parsnips in 2 or 3 batches.) Don't pile the strips high on the baking sheet—you want them in one loose messy layer, keeping in mind that it's okay if there is a bit of overlap. Sprinkle a light dusting of nutmeg over the parsnips. I'm a big fan of taking a whole nutmeg and using a Microplane to finely grate the spice.

Place the baking sheet into the hot oven. (There's no need to flip the crisps while they cook.) Start checking for doneness after 12 minutes—you know it's time to check when you can smell them roasting. You want your crisps to be light and golden when done. Feel free to pull out parsnips that look finished, and stick remaining strips back in the oven for a few minutes. Also keep in mind that your second batch will cook more quickly on the already hot baking sheet.

Generously sprinkle with sea salt and serve warm.

french lentils with preserved lemon, tarragon, and creamy goat cheese

I like a ton of goodies in my lentil salads. The crunch of carrots and celery is a nice contrast in texture with the tender legumes, while preserved lemon and tarragon add a playful range of flavor. I could eat these lentils anytime.

Quick-to-cook, and no soaking required, Du Puy lentils make a lovely side dish or a satisfying vegetarian main. Because this salad is best at room temperature and the Du Puy lentils really hold their shape, this is a great dish to make ahead for a luncheon or picnic.

serves 4 to 6

2 cups dried Du Puy lentils

1 dried bay leaf

Sea salt

1 cup chopped carrot

1 cup chopped celery

½ cup finely chopped shallot

5 tablespoons extra-virgin olive oil

2 tablespoons packed chopped Preserved Lemons (page 240), use the peels only and rinse to remove excess salty brine

2 tablespoons red wine vinegar

2–4 tablespoons fresh goat cheese

2 tablespoons fresh tarragon leaves

Rinse the lentils and place in a large saucepan or small stockpot with the bay leaf, 1 teaspoon salt, and 6 cups water. Gently simmer for 25 to 30 minutes, until tender. (Add additional water as needed to keep lentils covered in liquid.) Drain and let cool to room temp. Discard the bay leaf.

Cook the carrot, celery, and shallot with 2 tablespoons olive oil and a generous pinch of salt in a large skillet. After 6 to 8 minutes, when the veggies are just tender but still maintain a nice bite, take off the heat and let cool.

Once everything has come to room temp, stir the veggies and lentils together in a medium bowl. Mix in the chopped preserved lemon, vinegar, and the remaining 3 tablespoons olive oil. Season generously with sea salt. Taste for seasoning and add additional vinegar and olive oil as desired. Just before serving, scatter the goat cheese and tarragon over the salad.

avocado mama-style

A ripe avocado with a squeeze of lemon and a sprinkling of good salt is deeply satisfying for me and has been my go-to snack for as long as I can remember. My little girl continues this avocado-loving tradition. After school, when Lilah is desperate for a pick-me-up, she often asks, "Can I have an avocado Mama-style?" and I know just what to do.

This is less of a recipe and more of an acknowledgment that luscious raw ingredients often need only a whisper of attention to be transformed into a meal or really good snack. Advertisements and alluring packaging have us rushing to the supermarkets to buy all sorts of processed and packaged junk. If we can simply catch our breath and head to the produce aisle, there's a rainbow of natural goodness waiting to fill our bellies.

serves 1

1 ripe but firm Hass avocado

½ lemon

Pinch of good sea salt (Maldon is my favorite here)

Slice the avocado in half. Scoop out the pit. Squirt lemon juice over the naked avocado and sprinkle with salt. Get out a spoon and get snacking. Forget about the plate. Who needs it?

rainbow slaw with purple cabbage, green apple, radish, and orange

An untraditional California-style take on Mexican food is always a popular dinner option at our house. Soft corn tortillas, crème fraîche, a big pot of beans, maybe a little grilled meat, and this colorful slaw seems to please even the pickiest of eaters. The combination of purple cabbage strips, green apple batons, and pink-tinged radish slivers makes for a colorful, fresh, and crunchy addition to any Mexican spread. Eat the slaw packed into tacos, or go ahead and serve it as a vibrant side salad.

serves 6

2 Granny Smith apples

Juice of 2 limes

2½ cups shredded purple cabbage

6 or 7 small red radishes or 2 or 3 watermelon radishes, sliced into thin circles, then quartered

Juice of 2 oranges

3 tablespoons apple cider vinegar

2 tablespoons maple syrup

1 cup loosely packed chopped fresh cilantro

Sea salt

Thinly sliced jalapeño chile peppers (optional)

Leaving the skins on, cut the apples into matchstick-size batons and place them in a large bowl. Immediately toss the apple batons with the lime juice to keep them from browning. Add the cabbage and radishes. Squeeze the orange juice onto the veggies. Pour on the vinegar and maple syrup. Add the cilantro to the slaw. Sprinkle generously with sea salt and give everything a good toss with your hands.

Add extra salt, lime, maple syrup, or some jalapeño to your liking—you want the slaw to have a good fresh bite.

Let the flavors mingle at room temperature for at least half an hour before serving.

greens and beans

When it comes to making lunch for myself, I'm a bit of a scavenger. I like to take leftovers from the fridge and spice them up with a hearty portion of steamed greens. I've recently fallen in love with collards, and I'm thrilled to know they're packed with calcium and valuable antioxidants.

Seeing that we brew up a pot of beans on a weekly basis, one of my favorite lunches is a warm bowl of beans topped with steamed greens, hunks of avocado, and a citrusy dressing. A final addition of pepitas adds a nice crunch. This hippie meal-in-a-bowl suits me just fine—it's hearty, fresh, and nourishing all at the same time.

If you're looking to add some grains to your greens and beans, you can toss all of these ingredients onto a bed of brown rice or quinoa or into warm corn tortillas. Serve with a side of Quick-Pickled Onions (page 82) and Rainbow Slaw (page 76) for a more elaborate spread that could make for a vegetarian dinner as well.

....

serves 2

dressing:

4 teaspoons extra-virgin olive oil

2 teaspoons freshly squeezed lemon
  or lime juice

1 or 2 cloves garlic, finely chopped

Sea salt

greens:

1 large bunch collard greens (kale
  works here as well)

beans:

2 cups cooked black beans (to make
  your own, see The Simple Pleasure
  of a Pot of Beans, page 260) or
  1 (15-ounce) can

Sea salt

toppings:

1 avocado, cut into smallish chunks

¼ cup pepitas (see Tip on page 53)

2 lemon or lime wedges

Dash of hot sauce

Sea salt

Dollop of crème fraîche (optional; see
  page 266 for making your own)

Quick-Pickled Onions (optional;
  page 82)

For the dressing: Whisk together the oil, lemon juice, garlic, and salt in a large bowl. Set aside.

For the greens: Remove and discard the collard stems. Coarsely chop the leaves (you will have 5 to 6 cups chopped greens) and steam them for 5 to 10 minutes, until vibrant and tender. Transfer the steamed collards to the bowl of dressing and toss to coat.

For the beans: Warm the beans. Season with salt to taste.

Scoop the warm beans into shallow bowls. Next, put the dressed collards onto the beans. Top with chunks of avocado, a scattering of pepitas, another squeeze of citrus juice, and a dash of hot sauce, if you like it spicy. Season with another sprinkling of sea salt as desired, and top with crème fraîche and/or pickled onions, if you like.

skillet-fried potato coins in duck fat

My family wolfs down potatoes cooked this way. And why wouldn't they? Crispy, fluffy, salty spuds are irresistibly good. Cooking potato coins in decadent duck fat gives a depth of flavor and an extravagant bite to the whole affair.

Tip: You should be able to find rendered duck fat at gourmet grocers and specialty butcher shops. Whatever duck fat you don't use for the potato coins can be stored for months in the freezer.

serves 4

Sea or kosher salt

1 pound fingerling potatoes or small Yukon golds

¼ cup rendered duck fat

Freshly ground black pepper

Chopped fresh dill or flat-leaf parsley (optional)

Fill a large saucepan or small stockpot with water. Add salt generously, as you would for pasta water, and bring to a boil.

Boil the whole potatoes for 10 minutes. Drain and let the potatoes cool until they can be easily handled. Slice the potatoes into ⅛"-thick rounds (coins). Pat the potato rounds with paper towels to dry before frying.

Heat the duck fat in a large skillet over medium to medium-high heat. When the duck fat is nice and hot but not smoking, add enough potato rounds to cover the bottom of the pan. Cook for 3 to 5 minutes, until the undersides are golden but not too dark. Flip the coins and cook the other side until golden. Transfer the cooked potatoes to a plate lined with paper towels as you continue to batch-cook your potato rounds. Season generously with salt and pepper. Sprinkle on some freshly chopped herbs, if you want.

Serve immediately.

a pint of quick-pickled onions

These pretty pink onions are ridiculously easy to make and such a treat to have on hand. We serve them with burgers, tacos, pulled pork, fried chicken, a simple bowl of Greens and Beans (page 79), or a platter of smoked salmon with crackers and crème fraîche.

My boy, Otis, is such a fan of anything pickled that he'll eat these onions all by themselves as a snack, and I've caught him nibbling pickled onions for breakfast. They're that good!

makes 1 pint

1¾ cups apple cider vinegar

½ cup sugar

2 teaspoons kosher salt

1 teaspoon caraway seeds

1 teaspoon black peppercorns

2 dried bay leaves

1 medium red onion

Pint-size jar

Warm the vinegar, sugar, salt, caraway seeds, peppercorns, and bay leaves in a small saucepan. Simmer gently for 10 minutes, stirring occasionally to make sure the sugar fully dissolves.

Peel your onion, cut it in half, and slice it thinly. Pack as many onion slices as you can into a pint-size jar. Pour the hot liquid and all accompanying spices over the tops of the onion slices. Cover the jar and let everything cool to room temp, and you've got quick-pickled onions. Feel free to eat the onions as soon as they cool to room temp, but keep in mind that the flavor and color will only deepen a few days after pickling.

Tip: Store onions in a lidded container in the fridge for up to 2 weeks. When you've eaten all the onions, you can use the remaining pickling juice as a base for a zingy salad dressing.

roasted radicchio with medjool dates

For me, this dish sings of winter. We don't grow radicchio ourselves, but I love to see those gorgeous deep purples and speckled chartreuses gracing the winter farmers' market. In this dish, the bitter bite of wilted radicchio is counter-balanced with the caramelly sweetness of dates. The flavors here are strong and complex, yet making this wintery side dish couldn't be much quicker.

Roasted chicories make a flavorful side for any simple roasted chicken, lamb, steak, or brined pork chops. Vegetarian friends, try the chicories alongside a bowl of winter squash soup.

When I find both the standard Chioggia radicchio and the speckled variety (also known as Castelfranco), I like to mix the two chicories in this recipe.

serves 4

1½ pounds radicchio (2 large heads Chioggia radicchio or 4–6 heads Castelfranco)

2 tablespoons olive oil

Sea salt

3 or 4 Medjool dates, pitted and chopped

¼ cup roasted hazelnuts, roasted salted Marcona almonds, or toasted almond slivers (optional)

Preheat the oven to 450°F.

If you are roasting round, traditional radicchio, trim off the stem ends, peel off a layer of outer leaves, and cut each head into 6 wedges—don't worry if the leaves loosen up and the wedges are not intact. If you are using smaller heads of speckled radicchio, go ahead and quarter them. Place the radicchio onto a baking sheet and drizzle with the olive oil. Toss with your hands to coat. Sprinkle with salt.

Roast the radicchio in the hot oven, shaking the pan after a few minutes to ensure even cooking. Take the radicchio from the oven after 7 to 8 minutes of cooking, when it's tender, wilted, and just starting to char.

Toss with the chopped dates and the nuts, if you like, and serve immediately.

watercress salad with balsamic cherries

There's a romance to the bitter sweetness of this salad's ingredients. Sweet cherries and shallots soaked in balsamic vinegar are well matched to peppery watercress leaves. Mild fresh goat cheese and toasted hazelnuts ground the feisty and sumptuous union.

When fresh cherries aren't in season, you can use dried cherries. Simply rehydrate the dried cherries in warmed balsamic vinegar for 10 minutes, then use ¼ cup of this liquid to macerate the shallots and cherries as detailed below.

This salad is delish with grilled pork chops, steak, or duck.

serves 4

1 tablespoon very thinly sliced shallot

5 ounces fresh cherries (⅔ cup pitted cherries), halved

¼ cup balsamic vinegar

Maldon or other sea salt

4 large handfuls watercress (crisp butter lettuce is a milder and still delicious alternative)

¼ cup extra-virgin olive oil

⅓ cup coarsely chopped toasted hazelnuts or roasted salted Marcona almonds

2–3 ounces fresh goat cheese, crumbled

Freshly ground black pepper

Place the shallot and cherries in a small bowl, cover with the balsamic vinegar and a pinch of salt, and let macerate for about half an hour.

Scatter the watercress leaves onto 4 little plates.

Drain the cherries and shallot and scatter them over the watercress, being sure to save the flavorful liquid. Whisk 1½ tablespoons reserved liquid with the oil. Season the dressing with another pinch of salt. (Save the remaining balsamic liquid to use for future salad dressings.)

Sprinkle each salad with the nuts, goat cheese, and black pepper. Drizzle a little dressing over the top just before serving.

mushroom lovers' galette with herby goat cheese

Don't get me started talking about how happy a savory galette makes me, unless you want me to chatter away all day. I think of a savory galette as a welcome alternative to the ubiquitous pizza. A big pile of veggies always makes me smile, and tucking said veggies (along with cheese and herbs) into a flaky crust makes me giddy. Once you know how to make tart dough, you can bake up all sorts of deliciousness: Think tomato galettes in the summer, asparagus tarts in the spring, squash galettes in the winter. . . .

Make and chill the dough at least an hour before starting this recipe.

serves 3 or 4 as a main, or 6 to 8 as a side

2 tablespoons unsalted butter, divided

2 tablespoons olive oil, divided

1 pound cremini mushrooms, sliced ⅛" thick, divided

Sea salt

5 ounces fresh goat cheese

2 tablespoons fresh thyme leaves (use lemon thyme if possible)

1 portion Flaky Gluten-Free Pastry Dough (page 264)

1 egg yolk, whisked

Handful chopped fresh flat-leaf parsley leaves (optional)

Over medium heat, melt 1 tablespoon of the butter and 1 tablespoon of the oil in a large skillet. Cook half of the mushroom slices: Season generously with salt and cook for 3 to 5 minutes, stirring occasionally. You want your mushrooms to release their liquid and become tender and nicely browned. (Keep in mind that the mushrooms will cook further when they are baking in the galette.) Set the cooked mushrooms aside to cool while you cook the remaining mushrooms in the remaining 1 tablespoon butter and remaining 1 tablespoon oil. Drain off any excess liquid and set aside all of the cooked mushrooms.

Prepare the herby goat cheese: In a small bowl, use a fork to mix the goat cheese with the thyme leaves.

Once the mushrooms have cooled to room temp, assemble your galette. Preheat the oven to 375°F.

Roll out the dough to about $\frac{1}{8}$" thick, and place it on a parchment-lined baking sheet. Crumble a layer of herby goat cheese over the rolled-out dough, leaving 2" to 3" of free space around the border—this edge will get folded up and over the ingredients in just a minute. Next, lay the cooked mushrooms on top of the goat cheese. Now, fold the edges up and over the mushrooms. Brush the edges of the crust with the egg yolk and place the galette in the hot oven on the lowest rack.

Bake the galette for 40 minutes, or until the crust is golden and cooked on the bottom. Let cool for a few minutes. Top with the parsley just before serving, if you like.

veggie broth from scraps

If you are like me, you hate to discard any of the gorgeous veggies you've bought or grown. I think of the care the farmers (or sometimes we ourselves) have put into growing these vegetables from tiny seeds. I think of all the rainwater that has been slurped up. I think of the money we've earned and spent on this food. Whenever I toss perfectly good veggie scraps into the compost bin, I feel a tug at my conscience telling me the act is wrong.

If you collect vegetable scraps throughout the week, you will find yourself with more than enough materials to make a sumptuous veggie broth come Sunday. I'm talking about gathering up the tough green ends of leeks, that extra head of bok choy that wasn't needed last night, stems chopped from tender broccoli florets, an unused bunch of turnips and their greens, a wayward carrot, a lonely celery rib, and that extra onion half you didn't end up using for Thursday's supper.

Toss your clean veggie scraps into a big stockpot. Add a dried bay leaf. A few dozen peppercorns. A tablespoon of sea salt. Maybe a few cloves of garlic, or a shallot. Any extra herbs you've got lying around. Maybe a rind of Parmesan. Cover everything with plenty of water, nearly filling the pot. Bring the liquid to a boil, then turn the heat down to achieve a gentle simmer. Partially cover the pot and watch your scraps turn into nourishment after a few hours of simmering.

When the stock is infused with flavor, turn off the heat and let the liquid cool a bit. Use a slotted spoon to scoop the well-used veg right into the compost bin and strain the broth through a fine-mesh strainer.

Use your broth to make risottos, soups, stews—anything you crave. Stick any extra stock into lidded containers and freeze until you need it.

Tip: Avoid using carrot tops in your broth—I think they impart a bitter flavor.

caramelized brussels sprouts with a splash of saba

It's hard to believe that Brussels sprouts were once the pariah of the family dinner table. Gone are my childhood days of the dreaded boiled rounds with their odd odor and unappealing taste. Caramelized Brussels are now an extremely popular dish at our house, especially with a splash of decadent saba. When my kids beg me to cook Brussels sprouts, I smile to myself and happily roast up a big batch of this once-misunderstood veg.

A Note on Saba: If you haven't bought saba before, you may want to splurge on some at your local specialty food store. Saba, the result of slowly cooked grape must, is a thick, sweet, tangy syrup similar to a true aged balsamic vinegar. You need only a splash to transform something like simply roasted Brussels sprouts into a fancy-tasting dish. You can also use saba on winter squash, or roasted chicories, or in place of vinegar for an irresistible salad dressing. If you don't have access to saba or don't feel like splurging, as a substitute, you can simmer standard balsamic vinegar on the stove top until it becomes thick and concentrated.

....

serves 4

1 pound (4 cups) Brussels sprouts
2 tablespoons olive oil
Sea salt

1–2 tablespoons saba (available at
    most specialty grocers)
1 teaspoon apple cider vinegar

Preheat the oven to 425°F. Trim the stems off the Brussels sprouts and discard any funky outer leaves. Quarter large sprouts or halve smaller sprouts, and scatter them onto a baking sheet. Use your hands to toss the sprouts with the olive oil and salt. Transfer the pan to the hot oven.

    After 8 minutes, give the pan a shake and continue roasting the sprouts for 8 to 12 minutes, until the insides are tender and the edges are nicely browned. Remove from the oven and drizzle on the saba and vinegar. Sprinkle with a little more salt to taste. Toss and serve.

sea

bolinas crab pasta with citrus and mint

Every year around Thanksgiving, Dungeness crab season begins in Bolinas, the charming surf town where my mom lives, just north of San Francisco. Bolinas is one beautiful spot, and it's no wonder crabs plucked from those waters taste especially good. When we glimpse the fishermen dragging their seaweed-encrusted traps to the docks, we all wiggle with anticipation. We give thanks for those tasty crustaceans.

While we look forward to the yearly ritual of buying, cooking, and shelling fresh Bolinas crab, truly you don't need anything more than good-quality lump crabmeat for this recipe. If you buy the crab already cooked, cleaned, and shelled, this delectable dish can be thrown together in less than half an hour.

serves 4

1 package dried spaghetti {GF folks: see page xxi of "Stocking the Pantry" for suggestions}

6 tablespoons unsalted butter

¼ cup freshly squeezed lemon juice

½ pound cooked crabmeat

Plenty of sea salt

Freshly ground black pepper

Zest of 2 lemons

¼ cup chopped fresh mint leaves

Red-pepper flakes (optional)

1 lemon, quartered

Start by cooking your pasta. {Stir gluten-free pasta vigorously at the beginning of cooking to ensure the strands don't stick together.}

In the meantime, melt the butter in a large skillet over low heat. Add the lemon juice, then toss in the cooked crab and season generously with salt and pepper.

Drain the cooked pasta and add it to the large skillet. Stir the pasta to coat, cover, and let the flavors mingle for a few minutes before serving.

Scoop your pasta into shallow bowls. Top with the lemon zest, mint, a few more grinds of black pepper, and red-pepper flakes (if you like the spice). Give everyone his or her own lemon wedge to squeeze over the pasta, giving the dish one last splash of citrus brightness before taking a bite.

halibut baked in parchment + tarragon pesto

You can make this sumptuous supper in half an hour, maybe less. Parchment packets are super charming, with a celebratory, special-occasion vibe. If you want to make these for guests, go ahead; baking halibut in parchment is deceptively easy (with very little cleanup!) and makes for wonderfully moist fish and a quick weeknight dinner. Don't worry; I won't give away our secret if you won't.

This halibut is delicious served with Mixed Grains with Asparagus, Favas, Watercress, and Toasted Pine Nuts (page 187) or a citrusy risotto.

Tip: If you happen to have extra pesto at the end of the meal, use it to top poached eggs or a frittata, or swirl a scoop into a bowl of warm beans.

....

serves 4

tarragon pesto:

1 cup chopped fresh tarragon leaves, or a combination of fresh tarragon and flat-leaf parsley leaves

2 tablespoons toasted pine nuts or roasted salted Marcona almonds

1 small clove garlic, coarsely chopped

Zest of 1 lemon

1 teaspoon freshly squeezed lemon juice

Sea salt

2 tablespoons olive oil

halibut:

1¼ pounds halibut, cut into 4 fillets

Sea salt

1 tablespoon unsalted butter, cut into thin slivers

1 lemon, sliced into thin rounds

4 teaspoons water or white wine

Lemon wedges, for serving (optional)

Preheat the oven to 400°F.

First, make your pesto: If you have a mortar and pestle, use it to pulverize the chopped tarragon leaves, pine nuts, garlic, and lemon zest. You can also use a small food processor, or just chop all the ingredients like crazy. Add the lemon juice, a pinch of salt, and the olive oil. Combine and taste for seasoning, adding more lemon juice, salt, or olive oil to your liking. (I prefer this pesto to be coarse and chunky, but if you like a smoother pesto, feel free to add more olive oil.) Set the pesto aside while you bake the fish.

Prep the halibut: Cut four 12" squares of parchment paper and lay them on the counter or cutting board. Place a halibut fillet in the center of each paper. Sprinkle a generous pinch of sea salt onto each piece of fish and top with slivers of butter and 3 thin lemon rounds. Give each fillet a little splash of water or white wine, about a teaspoon per packet.

Wrap the parchment around each fillet in gift-wrap fashion, then tie kitchen twine around the packets to hold them closed. (Or you can crimp and tuck the edges of the paper together to create a closed packet.) Try not to wrap the parchment too tightly around the fish—you want to leave space for a pocket of steam to surround the fillet while it cooks.

Place the parchment packets on a baking sheet and bake for 15 to 20 minutes, until the halibut is opaque and flakes easily with a fork. (Baking time will vary with the thickness of the fillets. Don't feel shy about opening a packet to test for doneness. Simply wrap it again and return it to the oven if more cooking time is needed.)

For dramatic effect, you can serve the halibut fillets in their parchment packets. Open up the paper, scoop on some tarragon pesto, nestle in a lemon wedge if you want, and enjoy.

fish tacos topped with pomegranate salsa

Otis, our gregarious middle-schooler, loves his independence. He feels totally at ease roaming our Berkeley neighborhood with his buddies. At the end of every week, the dudes ride their bikes all over town to celebrate "Bro Friday." After an epic ride, the guys are starving, and sometimes the hungry hoard ends up at our house. Thanks to their time spent at the Edible Schoolyard, the "bros" are excellent helpers in the kitchen: They gamely whip up corn tortillas from scratch, and Otis had the idea for pomegranate salsa. Gotta love teenage boys who scarf fish tacos and love to cook!

These tacos make a fantastic meal on their own, or they can serve as a delectable part of a bigger spread. Warm black beans (see page 260 to make your own), Quick-Pickled Onions (page 82), and a simple arugula salad with Citrus Garlic Dressing (page 267) make for quite a feast. Fish tacos are a good way to feed any crowd of friends, family, or middle-school dudes.

....

serves 4

salsa:

1¼ cups fresh pomegranate seeds
(from 1 big pomegranate)

¼ cup freshly squeezed lime juice

2 tablespoons chopped fresh cilantro
(include the stems, where much of
the flavor resides)

2 tablespoons diced shallot or red
onion

1 jalapeño chile pepper, finely
chopped (optional)

Sea salt

fish:

3 tablespoons olive oil

Juice of 3 limes

Sea Salt

Freshly ground white pepper

1 pound tender white fish, like rock
cod or tilapia

for serving:

12 corn tortillas, warmed {GF folks:
check your labels; or, to make
your own corn tortillas from
scratch, see page 177}

½ cup crème fraîche (see page 266 for
making your own)

2 limes, quartered

Handful of fresh cilantro leaves

For the salsa: Combine the pomegranate seeds, lime juice, cilantro, shallot or onion, jalapeño (if desired), and salt to your liking. Let the flavors mingle for at least a half hour before serving.

Prep the fish: In a shallow bowl or baking dish, mix the olive oil, lime juice, a sprinkling of sea salt, and ground white pepper to taste. Give everything a stir and then add the fish fillets to the party. Let the fish marinate for 15 to 20 minutes only.

Heat a large skillet over medium-high heat. (I don't add any oil to the pan when I cook the fish. I make sure my skillet is nice and hot, and a little bit of oil from the marinade clings to the fish, keeping it from sticking.) Cook the fish for 2 to 3 minutes per side, until tender and flaky.

Serve the fish on warm corn tortillas, with the pomegranate salsa, a drizzle of crème fraîche, quartered limes, and a few cilantro leaves.

Tip: If you are a huge fan of pomegranates, you may want to consider doubling this salsa recipe.

wild salmon with dill butter + fennel

I spent the first decade of my life in Seattle, where deep pink, fatty wild king salmon was ubiquitous. The Pike Place Market wasn't just a touristy venture, but rather the place where we'd actually shop. Those famous fishmongers casually flung fish around in a way that seemed appropriate for such an abundant species. Elementary-school field trips took us to witness salmon heroically jumping up the locks. In those days, salmon steaks were on heavy rotation at our family's dinner table.

Considering what has happened to the wild salmon population in the past few decades, remembering the salmon plenty of my childhood feels like a foodie fairy tale. Now, we savor my favorite fish as the rare treat it has become.

In high summer, we love to serve this salmon with an *insalata caprese* and corn on the cob with a slathering of that dill butter, of course. A side of herby rice is also delish.

If you are one of the grilling ilk, feel free to grill the salmon and fennel—both ingredients are quite amenable to being prepared that way.

serves 4

dill butter:

4 tablespoons unsalted butter, softened

1 tablespoon finely chopped fresh dill

1 teaspoon finely chopped lemon zest

Pinch of sea salt

salmon + fennel:

1¼ pounds salmon, cut into 4 fillets

Sea salt

2 medium bulbs fennel

2–3 teaspoons olive oil

1 teaspoon chopped fresh dill

2 lemons, cut into wedges

First, prepare the herb butter: Use a fork to mix together the butter, dill, lemon zest, and salt. Wrap the herb butter in a piece of parchment or waxed paper, form a roll or log, and place it in the fridge to chill.

For the salmon: Season the salmon generously with salt and let the fish come to room temp for a half an hour before cooking.

When you're ready to cook, preheat the oven to 375°F.

For the fennel: Without discarding the core, slice the fennel bulb vertically into ¼"-thick slabs (each slice will look like a fan). Heat 2 teaspoons of the olive oil in a large cast-iron or ovenproof skillet over medium heat. Lay the fennel slices in the hot pan in a single layer. (You will need to cook the fennel in 2 or 3 batches. Add another splash of olive oil as needed.) Cook the fennel until lightly browned on both sides, allowing 4 to 6 minutes of cooking time for each side. Transfer the fennel to a serving platter, but keep your skillet on the stove top. You're going to cook the salmon in the pan with the remaining oil and those tasty little bits of browned fennel. (Gotta love a lack of dirty dishes!)

Top the caramelized fennel with the teaspoon of chopped dill, a squeeze of lemon juice, and a sprinkling of sea salt.

After finishing the fennel, make sure the heat under the skillet is still on medium. When the pan is nice and hot, place the salmon fillets in the pan, skin side down. Sear for 2 minutes, then pop the skillet into the hot oven to finish cooking the fish. If you like your salmon medium-rare (we do!), it will only need 6 to 9 minutes to cook, depending on the thickness of the fillets. Top each piece of salmon with a pat of herb butter right when it comes out of the oven.

Serve the salmon and fennel immediately, with additional lemon wedges.

Tip: You'll have plenty of extra herb butter to use on sweet corn or sautéed veg, or to make a batch of herby rice.

steamed mussels with rosé, leeks, and mustard

If you want a bowl of steaming hot goodness that tastes of the sea, mussels are for you. These bivalves are super quick to prepare and relatively inexpensive to buy considering what an impressive meal they make. The additions of mustard, garlic, and bay make for a pungent and flavorful bite. Plus mussels pass muster in the world of sustainable seafood, making my conscience as happy as my tastebuds. Serve with Polenta Fries (page 164) to sop up all the broth.

serves 4

3 pounds mussels in their shells, debearded

2 leeks

1 tablespoon olive oil

2 tablespoons unsalted butter

1 dried bay leaf

6 sprigs fresh thyme

12 black peppercorns

4 cloves garlic, thinly sliced

2 cups dry rosé or white wine

Pinch of sea salt

2 teaspoons Dijon mustard

¼ cup fresh flat-leaf parsley leaves, coarsely chopped

Place the mussels in a large colander, rinse under cold water, and set them aside while you prep the other ingredients.

Wash and trim the leeks. Thinly slice the white bulb end.

Heat the oil and butter in a large stockpot or Dutch oven over medium heat. Add the leeks, bay leaf, thyme, and peppercorns to the pot. Cook, covered over medium-low heat, until the leeks become translucent and tender. Add the garlic and cook for another minute. Next, add the wine and salt to the pot and turn the heat to high. Once the liquid is bubbling hot, add the mussels. Cover the pot and let those mussels steam. You'll know your mussels are done when they open up—this should take only 4 to 5 minutes of cooking. (If you end up with a couple of mussels whose shells won't open, discard them.)

Using a slotted spoon, scoop the mussels into shallow bowls. Whisk the mustard into the broth in the pot, then pour the hot liquid over each bowl of mussels. Finally, top with parsley leaves. Be sure to put an empty bowl on the table for discarding shells. Eat right away.

oysters with mignonette granita

Some of my favorite memories of Paul's and my early years together involve day trips to the coast, where we'd shuck and eat briny oysters just plucked from Tomales Bay. Over the years, we've honed our shucking skills and continue to slurp down platters of oysters whenever we get the chance. Our two kids are now enthusiastic partakers in our long-standing tradition. Otis and Lilah can down oysters with the best of 'em.

When we journey up to the oyster farm, we like to fill a little mason jar with mignonette to take along. A while back, a food-loving buddy mentioned the idea of mignonette granita. Brilliant, I thought. Now, when we bring a few dozen oysters back to our house, we eat the bivalves topped with little spoonfuls of rose-hued mignonette granita. The zesty ice makes me feel like I'm sitting by the bay with a layer of frost skimming the craggy shores.

serves anywhere from 2 to 6, depending on your appetite (makes ¾ cup granita)

½ cup champagne vinegar

¼ cup finely chopped shallot

2 teaspoons fresh thyme leaves (use lemon thyme if you can get it)

Few grinds black or white pepper

3–5 dozen fresh oysters

Whisk together the vinegar, shallot, thyme, and pepper. Pour into a freezer-proof shallow baking dish, place in the freezer. Use a fork to scrape the ice every 30 minutes until the entire mignonette is frozen and ready to serve. (Don't worry if you forget to scrape the granita as it freezes and it turns into a solid block of ice. You can scrape the hardened mignonette with a fork to still create a great texture.)

Shuck the oysters and rest them gently on the half-shell onto a platter of crushed ice. Use a small spoon to scoop a little spoonful of granita onto each oyster.

Slurp immediately.

Continued On Next Page

squid with lemon rounds, thyme sprigs, and big green olives

By now, everyone is quite familiar with fried calamari, but many of us never think to cook squid at home. Maybe we just don't know what to do with it.

Squid is a great sustainable seafood option and is usually well priced, especially when compared with its pricey neighbors at the seafood counter. Plus it's easy and extremely quick to cook! This simple recipe packs a nice range of flavors and textures: Juicy green olives and tons of lemon make every bite fresh and full of zing. Be sure to eat the cooked lemon rounds . . . they're delish.

Serve on top of lemony quinoa or rice, with a side of sautéed spinach or a simple leafy salad.

serves 4

1¼ pounds cleaned squid

4 lemons

3 tablespoons olive oil

⅔ cup big green olives
(Castelvetranos are amazing!)

6–8 sprigs fresh thyme

Sea salt

Freshly ground black or white pepper

Wash the squid in a colander under cool tap water, dry with paper towels, and cut the bodies into 1" rounds. There's no need to chop the tentacles unless they are large. Set the prepped squid aside.

Slice 2 of the lemons into thin rounds. Cut the remaining 2 lemons in half to squeeze over the cooked squid. Set aside.

Heat the oil in a large skillet over the highest possible heat. When the oil is really hot and just beginning to smoke, add the lemon rounds and let them sizzle for 30 seconds. Then add the squid, olives, and thyme. Stir regularly to ensure even cooking and make sure to keep the heat really high. (Quick, high-heat cooking is essential to ensuring that the squid is tender.)

With plenty of breathing room, squid can cook in as little as 90 seconds. In a crowded pan, it will still take only 2 to 3 minutes. Like shrimp, squid goes from translucent to opaque once it's done. When the squid is finished, squeeze on plenty of lemon juice from the lemon halves, season generously with salt, and crack on some freshly pepper. Serve immediately. Squid waits for no one.

black cod with grapefruit ginger marinade

Black cod, also known as sablefish, swim off the shores of California, and when we're lucky the fishermen bring these wild-caught beauties to market for us to enjoy. A rich, flaky fish, black cod can stand up to a flavorful marinade. Here a soulful undertone of sesame oil and the brightness of grapefruit and ginger give a fresh contrast to the buttery fillets. We always think of lemons and limes as great friends to seafood, yet grapefruit—a less common flavor—lends an element of surprise to this dish.

I cooked this black cod for my neighbors a while back, and their son, Aidan, who doesn't usually like fish at all, ate with delight. He came back for seconds, even thirds. I think it's the luscious marinade that won him over.

Serve this cod on a bed of rice: White, black, or brown works here. Be sure to drizzle the extra marinade over the rice.

serves 4

1¼ pounds black cod, sliced into 4 fillets

Sea or kosher salt

⅔ cup freshly squeezed grapefruit juice

¼ cup sesame oil

1 tablespoon gluten-free tamari

1 teaspoon grated fresh ginger

1 heaping teaspoon honey

1 clove garlic, finely chopped

1 grapefruit, cut into narrow wedges

Generously season the fish with salt when you bring it home from the market. It can rest, covered in the refrigerator, for a few hours or even overnight.

Come cooking time, whisk together the grapefruit juice, sesame oil, tamari, ginger, honey, and garlic in a shallow baking dish. Add the fish and marinate for only 20 to 30 minutes before cooking.

Remove the cod from the marinade, place the fillets on a baking sheet, and let them rest there for 10 minutes while you simmer the marinade. Transfer the marinade to a small saucepan and simmer vigorously for 7 to 10 minutes to reduce the marinade.

Meanwhile, crank up your broiler.

Place the cod 3" to 4" beneath the broiler and broil for 4 minutes. Brush each fillet generously with the reduced marinade and return the fish to the broiler for another 1 to 3 minutes, until the cod is flaky and cooked through. (Cooking time will vary depending on the thickness of your fillets.)

Serve the black cod with another drizzle of the reduced marinade and wedges of grapefruit. Place the remaining sauce in a small pitcher to be passed around the table.

prawns on lemongrass skewers

We first tasted these delightful prawns on Gili Trawangan, a sandy, idyllic wisp of an island in the Indonesian archipelago. Pip, a talented, bowler-hatted Indonesian chef, grilled these prawns for us on the beach one evening just after sunset, and we feasted by candlelight. (I kid you not.) I still have to pinch myself to believe we were lucky enough to experience such beauty and deliciousness during our family's year away. Every bite of this dish reminds me of this dreamy time, and I can tell you that Pip's soulful flavors can be harnessed and enjoyed in our kitchen across the globe.

I highly recommend serving these prawns with Pip's Yellow Rice (page 174) and a simple green salad.

Tip: If you don't want to bother tracking down fresh lemongrass, marinate the prawns with the ingredients below and cook them in a hot skillet, then top 'em with the onions, chiles, honey, lime wedges, and cilantro. The presentation won't be quite as festive, but the flavors will still be amazing.

....

serves 4

skewers:

8–10 stalks fresh lemongrass

marinade:

Juice of 2 limes

2 tablespoons canola oil

5 cloves garlic, coarsely chopped

1–2 tablespoons coarsely chopped
    fresh ginger

1 teaspoon sea salt

⅛ teaspoon freshly ground black
    pepper

prawns:

2 pounds prawns or large shrimp,
    peeled and deveined, tails still
    intact

2 or 3 limes

for serving:

2 tablespoons thinly sliced spring
    onions/scallions

1 tablespoon sliced chile peppers

1–2 tablespoons golden honey,
    warmed to a runny consistency

Freshly ground black pepper

Lime wedges

¼ cup chopped fresh cilantro leaves

Peel the outside layer off the lemongrass stalks and trim both ends. Use the side of a knife to bruise the firm white ends of the lemongrass to help release its fragrance. Set aside.

For the marinade: In a rectangular baking dish (large enough to accommodate the lemongrass skewers), combine the lime juice, oil, garlic, ginger, salt, and pepper.

Use a knife to make a little hole in each prawn for the lemongrass stalk to penetrate. Slide 3 or 4 prawns onto each stalk. Rub the marinade all over the skewered prawns and let them marinate for 1 hour at room temp.

Prepare a grill for high-heat cooking. Grill the prawn skewers for 2 to 3 minutes per side, keeping in mind that prawns turn opaque when cooked. Squeeze the juice of 2 or 3 limes over the prawns while cooking.

Top your cooked prawns with spring onions, chile peppers, drizzled honey, black pepper, and squeezes of plenty of additional lime wedges. Scatter the cilantro over the prawns and serve right away.

butcher shop

oven-roasted pork with fennel seeds, garden rosemary, and garlic rub

A pork loin roasted with a flavorful rub is an incredibly easy meal to whip up for a simple weeknight supper, or you can serve the juicy pork as a low-stress main for a dinner party. Plus your kitchen will fill with a heavenly smell of fennel seeds, rosemary, and garlic as the pork roasts in the oven. Paul and I always have our fingers crossed for leftovers—slices of pork loin make a happy lunch the next day.

This roast is super versatile and can accommodate all sorts of sides, from sautéed spinach to caramelized Brussels sprouts to roasted radicchio. And you can't go wrong with mashed potatoes.

serves 4

1½ pounds boneless pork loin (a bone-in roast also works, though additional cooking time will be needed)

Sea salt

2½ tablespoons fennel seeds

2 tablespoons chopped fresh rosemary

2 tablespoons finely chopped garlic

Freshly ground black pepper

2 tablespoons olive oil

Remove the pork from the fridge 45 minutes before cooking to allow the meat to come to room temperature. Pat dry, season the loin generously with salt, and set aside.

Preheat the oven to 375°F.

Crush the fennel seeds with a mortar and pestle or stick the seeds in a paper bag and whack with a meat tenderizer. (I prefer not to grind the fennel, but to crush the seeds just enough to release their aroma. If you like a finer grind, that works too; use a clean coffee grinder.)

Place the crushed fennel in a shallow bowl big enough to hold the pork loin. Add the rosemary, garlic, ½ teaspoon salt, some pepper, and the olive oil. Integrate the ingredients, and you've got your rub. Roll the loin in the rub to coat all sides thoroughly.

Preheat a medium cast-iron pan or other ovenproof skillet on the stove top over medium-high heat. (There's no need to add oil to the pan; the oil in the rub should do the trick.) Once the pan is nice and hot, brown all sides of the loin (4 to 5 minutes per side). Place the skillet in the hot oven and roast the pork for 25 to 35 minutes. Check for doneness with a meat thermometer—it should read 135° to 140°F when the pork is finished. Keep a close eye on the roast: It can go from undercooked to overcooked very quickly. Cooking time will vary with the size and thickness of the cut. Start checking after 20 minutes. If you are working with bone-in pork, the cooking time will be longer, of course. Just remember, you'll know it's done when a thermometer stuck deep into the roast reads 135° to 140°F.

Let the roast rest, loosely draped with aluminum foil, for 15 minutes before slicing and serving. Cooked this way, pork loin is juicy, slightly pink in the center, and oh so good.

cozy winter soup with fennel sausage, leeks, white beans, and rapini

Once autumn arrives and the cool weather and dark evenings take over, I crave a hearty one-bowl supper to warm my spirit. I make some version of this nourishing and flavorful soup throughout the colder months, and I always have leftovers in mind. I like to make this soup on a quiet Sunday, then tuck individual servings into the fridge or freezer for quick belly-warming lunches to last throughout the week. The flavors continue to deepen over the following days.

Tips: To make your own beans and chicken stock from scratch, see pages 260 and 148 for recipes. Start soaking your beans the night before. And save the leek tops and other veggie scraps to make a veggie broth (page 90).

. . . .

serves 8 to 10 (makes 4 quarts)

2 leeks

2 tablespoons unsalted butter

2 tablespoons olive oil

1 cup diced celery

1 cup diced yellow onion

1 cup diced carrots

1 dried bay leaf

Sea salt

1¼ pounds pork or turkey sweet Italian sausages with fennel {GF folks: please check your packaging, or ask the butcher to make sure sausages are gluten-free}

7 cups chicken stock (see tips)

1½ cups stewed tomatoes plus 2 tablespoons tomato paste (or 1½ cups chopped Candied Tomatoes, page 50, if you've got 'em)

2 large bunches rapini, woody stem ends removed, chopped, 6–8 cups (kale, collards, or any hearty leafy green would also work here)

1 (15-ounce) can cannellini beans or 2 cups beans made from scratch (see tips)

Freshly ground black pepper

for serving:

Chopped fresh flat-leaf parsley, grated Parmesan, and red-pepper flakes

Wash and trim the leeks. Slice the tender white ends into thin rounds—you want to have about 1 cup sliced leeks.

Melt the butter with the olive oil in a large stockpot or Dutch oven over medium heat. Add the leeks, celery, onion, carrots, bay leaf, and 1 teaspoon salt. Cover the pot and stew the veggies over medium-low heat until tender, 15 to 20 minutes.

In the meantime, in a large skillet, brown all sides of the fennel sausage—no need to fully cook the sausages at this point, because they will continue cooking in the stew. Remove the sausages from the heat and slice into ½"-thick rounds.

Once the stewing veggies are tender, add the chicken broth and tomatoes to the pot. Bring to a simmer and add the rapini and sausage rounds. Cook until both veggies and sausage are cooked through, about 8 more minutes of simmering.

Finally, add the beans to the pot. Turn off the heat and let all the ingredients mingle. Taste for seasoning and add salt and black pepper to your liking. (How much seasoning you'll need will depend on how salty your broth and sausages are.) I like red-pepper flakes in this stew, but I tend to serve them on the side so that the non-spicy members of my tribe enjoy the soup as well. Fish out and discard the bay leaf.

Scoop the stew into large shallow bowls and scatter chopped parsley over the top. Pass around bowls of grated Parm and red-pepper flakes.

succulent lamb chops nestled in fresh fig leaves + lemon cucumber tzatziki

This recipe is inspired as much by smell as by taste. Within minutes of placing the lamb in the hot oven, your kitchen will be filled with the earthy aroma of baking fig leaves. This scent instantly transports me to the Greek islands, where arid hills are dotted with fig trees warmed by the blazing Mediterranean sun. Maybe it's my Greek heritage, but the wild perfume of roasting fig leaves is magic to me.

Fresh fig leaves aren't the easiest things to find outside of California, but rest assured that this recipe is totally delectable without them. Follow all directions below, and when it comes to finishing the chops in the oven, just place the lamb directly in a baking dish or ovenproof skillet. You may miss out on the scent of baking fig leaves, but you'll still be rewarded with the taste of succulent chops.

My kids claim that they don't even like lamb, yet they devour chops prepared this way!

Marinate your lamb, and make your tzatziki, a few hours before you want to cook.

....

serves 3 or 4

marinade and lamb:

2 tablespoons olive oil

1 teaspoon freshly squeezed lemon juice

1 tablespoon chopped fresh rosemary

3 cloves garlic, minced

2 pounds double-thick rib lamb chops
(2 ribs per chop)

for cooking and serving:

4–6 fresh fig leaves (optional)

Flaky sea salt

Freshly ground black pepper

Lemon wedges

tzatziki:

½ cup plain yogurt

½ cup peeled, seeded, and finely
chopped cucumber

1 or 2 cloves garlic, pressed or finely
chopped

1–2 teaspoons freshly squeezed
lemon juice

A dozen fresh mint leaves or dill
fronds, chopped

Sea salt

Freshly ground black pepper

At least 2 hours before serving, assemble your marinade by combining the olive oil, lemon juice, rosemary, and garlic. Place the lamb in a glass container and coat with the marinade. Cover and refrigerate. One hour before cooking, remove lamb from the fridge to allow meat to return to room temp.

Also try to make the tzatziki ahead of time: In a small bowl, mix together the yogurt, cucumber, garlic, lemon juice, chopped herbs, and salt and pepper to taste. Let the sauce chill in your fridge. Tzatziki only gets better as the flavors mingle.

When you're ready to cook your lamb, preheat the oven to 400°F.

Place a large cast-iron skillet on the stove top over medium-high heat. When the pan is nice and hot but not quite smoking, brown all sides of the chops, 4 to 5 minutes per side. (I don't find it necessary to add any additional oil to the pan for browning, as some oil from the marinade will still be clinging to the chops.) To ensure a good sear, take care not to crowd the meat during this phase; brown the chops in batches if necessary.

Line a shallow baking dish with fig leaves, if you have them. Nestle the seared chops in the leaves. Place the baking dish in the hot oven to finish cooking the lamb. In minutes, your kitchen will be filled with the aroma of roasting fig leaves. Depending on the thickness of your chops, they may be done after only a few minutes in the oven, and shouldn't need more than 15 minutes. I have come to rely on touch testing my meat for doneness. There is that feeling of just the right give when meat is medium-rare. If you trust your fingers, go for it. Also feel free to use a meat thermometer: The chops will be juicy medium-rare when the internal temp reads 130° to 135°F. Let the chops rest for 10 to 15 minutes before serving.

Season the chops with flaky sea salt and generous grinds from the pepper mill. Serve the lamb in the baking dish with the fig leaves still underneath. Toss some lemon wedges into the dish so that everyone can squeeze the juice over the chops. Pass tzatziki around the table, and feel free to scoop it right onto the chops if you wish.

chicken thighs slathered in homemade bbq sauce

It's fun to make barbecue sauce from scratch, breathe in the array of toasting spices, and transform plain chicken thighs into a delectable dinner classic. This barbecue sauce is a "kitchen sink" recipe, or maybe just a "spice cupboard" recipe—all sorts of flavors get bubbled together in one smoky caramelized brew. I think you'll be surprised at just how many of these spices may already live in your spice rack.

This recipe makes enough sauce for a couple of meals, and you can make it anytime to have on hand, storing the sauce in the fridge for a few weeks. Of course, you can use your leftovers for another night of barbecue chicken, or go ahead and slop the sauce onto ribs, burgers, whatever your barbecue-loving heart desires.

serves 4 (makes 2½ cups sauce)

bbq sauce:

½–1 teaspoon ground cayenne pepper (adjust amount depending on your love of spice)

1 teaspoon smoked paprika, also known as *pimentón ahumado*

½ teaspoon mustard seeds, crushed

½ teaspoon ground cumin

¼ teaspoon ground turmeric

¼ teaspoon ground nutmeg

2 cups pureed/strained tomatoes

¼ cup tomato paste

½ cup molasses

½ cup pomegranate molasses (you can substitute ⅓ cup balsamic vinegar here)

⅓ cup honey

¼ cup apple cider vinegar

2 tablespoons balsamic vinegar

⅓ cup firmly packed light brown sugar

2 teaspoons sea salt

3 cloves garlic, minced

chicken:

6–8 chicken thighs, bone-in and skin-on

Salt

Freshly ground black pepper

To make the sauce: Toast all dry spices—cayenne pepper, smoked paprika, crushed mustard seeds, cumin, turmeric, and nutmeg—in a medium saucepan over medium heat for 3 to 4 minutes. You want the spices to release their flavors but not become burned.

Add the tomatoes, tomato paste, molasses, pomegranate molasses, honey, vinegars, brown sugar, salt, and garlic to the saucepan. Give everything a good stir and bring to a boil. Lower to a simmer and let the brew cook, uncovered, until everything reduces significantly, 30 to 45 minutes. Your sauce should be thick, caramelized, and smoky. Add additional salt to taste.

When you're ready to bake the chicken, preheat the oven to 400°F.

Season each chicken thigh generously with salt and black pepper. Heat a large skillet over medium-high heat. (Keep in mind: The chicken skin has plenty of fat and you shouldn't need to add oil to the pan before browning.) Brown skin side first, then flip to brown the other side. Do the browning in a couple of batches—you don't want to crowd the chicken. Then transfer the thighs to a large ovenproof baking dish, placing them skin side up.

Transfer the chicken to the hot oven. While the chicken is cooking, gently warm 1 cup of the sauce in a small saucepan.

After the chicken has cooked for 20 minutes, check for doneness with a meat thermometer. You want to register 165° to 170°F. (Return the pan to the oven if the chicken needs a little more cooking.) When the chicken is cooked through, pull the pan from the oven and turn on the broiler. Slather the skin of each thigh with sauce (use ½ to ¾ cup of sauce for slathering, and save the remaining sauce to serve with the meal). Place the pan under the broiler for a minute or two, until the saucy skin is bubbling and caramelized.

Serve the chicken thighs with a small bowl of warmed sauce for anyone who wants a little more.

Tip: Leftover barbecue sauce can be stored in a lidded container in the fridge for up to 2 weeks.

juicy burgers with gruyère, avocado, and pickled onions, tucked into butter lettuce "buns"

When I spend big bucks for high-quality beef, I don't need to weigh my burger down with a bready bun. Yes, there are plenty of decent gluten-free hamburger buns, but we prefer to eat our burgers wrapped in crisp butter lettuce. When serving burgers this way, the meat takes center stage, just as it should.

We often serve burgers with a side of Parsnip Crisps (page 71). And of course, you can add the condiments of your choice: Ketchup, mustard, and Sriracha mayo are favorites at our house.

serves 4

1¼ pounds ground beef

1 teaspoon kosher salt

Freshly ground black pepper

3 ounces Gruyère cheese, grated
(sharp Cheddar is also good)

1 avocado

1 head butter lettuce, leaves separated

½ cup Quick-Pickled Onions
(page 82)

Let the meat come to room temperature for 30 minutes before forming the burger patties.

Always keep in mind that the key to a tender burger is to very lightly handle your ground beef. Sprinkle the beef with salt and black pepper. Gently form four 1"-thick patties.

Prepare a grill for high-heat cooking. Grill the patties over high heat for 3 to 4 minutes on the first side. Flip and top with the grated cheese. Cook for 3 to 4 minutes on the second side for medium-rare burgers.

Let the cooked burgers rest for 5 minutes before serving. Pit, peel, and thinly slice your avocado. At serving time, nestle each patty into a large leaf of butter lettuce. Top with avocado slices, pickled onions, and plenty of ground black pepper.

Eating burgers this way is a bit messy, but my gang doesn't seem to mind an excuse to lick their fingers clean.

bourbon-braised short ribs with brown sugar and coffee

This is lavish winter fare. Here we braise short ribs in an ambrosia of coffee, bourbon, brown sugar, and orange—we are talking dark, rich, bone-warming decadence. Serve the succulent ribs on a bed of creamy polenta or mashed potatoes and all you'll need is a simple salad or lemony sautéed spinach on the side. These ribs make a great dish to serve to dinner guests.

Don't forget to slather the ribs in the rub and let them sit overnight before cooking. And keep in mind that you can make these ribs up to 3 days before serving, as the flavors deepen and become even more blended and enriched with time. To make the dish in advance, fully cook the ribs and store them in their braising liquid in a covered container in the fridge. Before serving, skim off as much fat as possible from the sauce. Re-warm the ribs by braising in a covered pan in a 350°F oven for 30 to 40 minutes. Transfer the ribs to a baking sheet for quick broiling, and simmer the sauce for a few minutes as per the finishing instructions below.

Tip: It is essential to use the right salt for this recipe. If you substitute sea salt or regular table salt here, you will need to reduce the amount of salt accordingly. Diamond kosher salt is milder and less "salty" than the alternatives. Also be sure to use low-sodium beef broth.

serves 4

dry rub and ribs:

2 tablespoons light or dark brown sugar

1 tablespoon finely ground coffee

4 teaspoons Diamond kosher salt (see tip)

½ teaspoon ground cayenne pepper

Plenty of freshly ground black pepper

3½–4 pounds beef short ribs

the braise:

1 tablespoon canola oil

3 cups low-sodium beef broth

½ cup brewed coffee

¼ cup bourbon

5 cloves garlic, slivered

Zest and juice of 1 orange

Couple of splashes Worcestershire sauce

Maldon or other sea salt

The night before: Combine the brown sugar, ground coffee, salt, cayenne pepper, and black pepper. Rub all over the ribs, cover, and refrigerate.

On cooking day: Remove the ribs from the fridge and let them sit for 1 hour to come to room temperature.

Preheat the oven to 325°F.

In a wide heavy-bottom skillet, heat the oil over medium-high heat. Brown the ribs on all sides; 3 to 4 minutes per side is all you'll need, as the sugar in the rub helps the ribs caramelize quickly. You will want to do the browning in batches so as not to overcrowd the pan. (Allow yourself 20 to 30 minutes for browning.) Transfer the browned ribs to a roasting pan or large Dutch oven while you prepare the braising liquid.

Add the broth, coffee, bourbon, garlic, orange zest, orange juice, and a couple of splashes of Worcestershire to the skillet, and use a whisk to scrape up all the browned bits from the pan. Bring the liquid to a boil and simmer for 2 minutes. Pour the hot liquid over the ribs. Tightly cover the pan with aluminum foil (or the Dutch oven with its lid) and put it in the hot oven.

After 1½ hours, flip the ribs over. (Be careful when you lift the foil—it's steamy.) Cover again and cook the ribs for 1½ to 2 hours. You'll know the ribs are done when the meat is tender and falling from the bone. Pull the cooked ribs from the pan and place them on a baking sheet. Turn the oven to broil.

Skim off as much fat as possible from the braising liquid and pour the liquid into a saucepan. Simmer the sauce for a few minutes to reduce it just a bit.

Sprinkle the ribs with sea salt and broil for a minute or two on each side to ensure a caramelized finish on the meat. If you so desire, feel free to remove the bones and excess fat from the ribs, and shred the meat before serving. Or you can simply nestle the warm ribs onto a bed of polenta or mashed potatoes, drizzle on plenty of sauce, and enjoy!

pork ragù with candied tomatoes

Now this is comfort food! It's no wonder so many people love a good meaty red sauce. My husband, Paul, is crazy about ragù—anytime he sees it on a restaurant's menu, he has to have it. When I started cooking ragù at our house, Paul was thrilled and so was I. This is the kind of sauce you can brew up on a lazy Sunday, and you've got the foundation for a quick and comforting homemade dinner once the busy week begins.

Candied Tomatoes (page 50) bring a magically rich depth of flavor to this ragù. You can substitute crushed tomatoes and tomato paste, but I cannot guarantee the ragù will be quite as ridiculously good.

Serve the ragù over a bed of Parmesan Polenta (page 166) or on top of your favorite pasta. I also enjoy eating ragù tossed with chopped-up artichoke hearts that I've quickly sautéed in olive oil.

Tip: When chopping garlic, add a pinch of salt. It makes the garlic less sticky and the whole task easier.

serves 4 to 6

¼ pound pancetta or bacon, diced

¼ cup finely chopped carrot

¼ cup finely chopped onion

¼ cup finely chopped celery

Bouquet garni: 1 sprig fresh sage, 1 sprig fresh rosemary, 3 sprigs fresh thyme, 2 sprigs fresh flat-leaf parsley, and 1 dried bay leaf tied with kitchen twine

1 pound ground pork

Kosher salt

Freshly ground black pepper

4 cloves garlic, minced

1 cup dry white wine

1 cup chopped Candied Tomatoes (page 50), or 2 cups crushed tomatoes plus ¼ cup tomato paste

⅓ cup whole milk

¼ cup grated Parmesan

2 tablespoons chopped fresh flat-leaf parsley

In a large heavy pot or Dutch oven, cook the pancetta or bacon over medium heat, stirring, for 8 to 10 minutes, until the meat is golden brown and starting to crisp. Add the carrot, onion, celery, and bouquet garni. Cook for 5 minutes, until the veggies are becoming translucent.

Add the ground pork, ½ teaspoon salt, and plenty of black pepper. Stir to integrate and cook for 5 minutes. Finally, add the garlic, wine, and tomatoes to the pot. Turn up the heat so everything cooks vigorously for 5 minutes and the wine reduces. Partially cover the pan, turn the heat down as low as possible, and maintain a gentle simmer. Cook for 2 hours, adding a tablespoon of the milk every 20 minutes and giving the brew a stir. Discard the bouquet garni. Season with additional salt and freshly ground pepper, as desired.

Transfer the ragù to a lidded container and refrigerate for up to 3 days before serving. The flavors just get better and better. At serving time, don't forget that final sprinkling of grated Parmesan and chopped parsley on top.

Freeze any leftover ragù for later use.

deconstructed california cobb

We are huge fans of the deconstructed salad at our house. Having separate components enticingly tucked into separate bowls appeals to picky eaters and allows everyone to eat just what he or she wants.

Arugula and fennel bulb are my unorthodox additions to the classic Cobb; I love the crisp crunch of fennel slivers and peppery bite of arugula. If you have access to fennel or arugula blossoms, toss them in too. The little flowers are so charming, and they give a nice kick of flavor.

This recipe can easily feed a family of four, or it can be doubled or tripled to feed a crowd.

serves 4

dressing:

1 heaping teaspoon Dijon mustard

2 tablespoons balsamic vinegar

⅓–½ cup extra-virgin olive oil

Sea salt

salad:

½ pound pan-fried or grilled chicken breast, torn into small pieces and seasoned with salt and pepper

½ pound bacon, crisp-cooked and broken into bite-size pieces

2 hard-boiled eggs, sliced into thin rounds or chopped

2 avocados, pitted, peeled, and sliced

½ cup thinly sliced fennel

¼ cup crumbled blue cheese {GF folks: check with the producers to be sure the cheese is gluten-free; or you could use a creamy fresh goat cheese as a safe substitute here}

1 cup cherry tomatoes, halved

Fennel or arugula blossoms (optional)

8 cups arugula or torn butter lettuce leaves

For the dressing: Whisk together the mustard, vinegar, oil, and salt to taste, and set aside.

Place the chicken, bacon, eggs, avocados, fennel, cheese, tomatoes, and blossoms (if using) in their own bowls. Place the bowls in the center of your dining table.

In a large salad bowl, lightly dress the salad greens. Pour the remaining dressing into a small pitcher and place it on your now-crowded table.

Set out 4 dinner plates or shallow bowls. Let everyone dig into the ingredients, creating a salad to their liking. Pass the dressing for an extra drizzle to top the goodies. Crack some black pepper over your salad and sprinkle with salt.

hanger steak with gremolata

Years ago, my French uncle, Jean Louis, turned us on to the delectable hanger steak, and we've been buying these beauties ever since. Hanger steak, sometimes called *onglet*, is a lesser known cut of beef, but butchers have long been hip to its great flavor and lovely marbling. It's no surprise that you'll sometimes find hanger steak referred to as "butcher's steak." A quick stint on the grill and a rub of brightly flavored gremolata make this steak an easy and flavorful weeknight dinner option. We often eat hanger steak with a big helping of Old School Caesar (page 56) on the side.

Tip: If you can't get hanger steak from your local butcher, a juicy rib eye is delicious grilled and topped with gremolata.

serves 4

1–1¼ pounds hanger steak

Salt

¼ cup chopped fresh flat-leaf parsley

1 tablespoon finely chopped lemon
    zest

2 cloves garlic, minced

Olive oil, as needed

Freshly ground black pepper

Remove the steak from the fridge 45 minutes before cooking. Season the meat generously with salt and let it come to room temp.

In a small bowl, toss together the parsley, lemon zest, garlic, 1 teaspoon olive oil, and a pinch of salt. Give the ingredients a good stir, taste for seasoning, and you've got your gremolata ready to roll.

Prepare a grill for medium-high heat. Pat the steak dry and rub with olive oil. Grill for 5 to 7 minutes per side; you want hanger steak to be medium-rare, or it can get tough. Pull the steak off the grill and immediately season with another light sprinkling of salt and some freshly ground pepper. Rub with the gremolata and let the steak rest for 10 to 15 minutes. Slice the steak thinly and against the grain.

butcher shop

pistachio kebabs on rosemary skewers

Istanbul is a city that loves to eat. We visited a few years ago and fell in love with the place. Wandering the old neighborhoods, we found old-fashioned food vendors everywhere: We bought orange juice squeezed fresh to order, almonds still in their shells, and even popcorn popped by an ancient hand crank. A food lover's paradise!

Almost every day we'd try a new delicious kebab—I was thrilled by this delectable gluten-free option. One of my favorite kebabs included chopped pistachios, and this recipe is a thanks to our time in Istanbul and a nod to the heavenly flavors of that magnificent city. Lemon Cucumber Tzatziki (page 122) is a great accompaniment.

Tip: It's best if you can prepare and mix your kebab ingredients 1 to 2 hours before cooking time, so the flavors can mingle.

....

serves 4

2 tablespoons finely chopped
   yellow onion

1 tablespoon olive oil

1 teaspoon ground cumin

Sea salt

1¼ pounds ground meat, preferably
   a mix of ¾ pound lamb and
   ½ pound beef

½ cup chopped fresh flat-leaf parsley

⅓ cup chopped roasted salted
   pistachios

Freshly ground black pepper

4 (12") rosemary branches or
   standard wood or metal skewers

In a small skillet over medium heat, cook the onion in the olive oil with the cumin and a pinch of salt until the onions are nice and soft. Transfer the cooked onions to a small bowl and be sure to let them cool completely before mixing with the raw meat. (I will even pop the bowl of onions into the fridge for a few minutes to speed the cooling process while I prep the other ingredients.)

In a large bowl, use your hands to gently mix the onions, ground meat, parsley, chopped pistachios, 1 teaspoon salt, and some black pepper. Transfer the meat to a covered container and refrigerate for at least an hour or two, or even overnight. Remove the meat from the fridge a half an hour before cooking so that everything comes to room temp before grilling.

Prepare a grill for medium-high heat cooking.

Prepare the rosemary skewers by removing almost all of the rosemary leaves from the branches, except for a few at the tip. Soak the branches in water for 10 to 15 minutes before skewering the meat—this will keep the skewers from catching fire. (Do this if you are using wood skewers, too.)

Use your hands to mold the ground meat around each skewer, kind of like a sausage without casing.

Grill the kebabs for a total of 7 to 8 minutes, rotating to cook evenly, until medium-rare.

bali garden stew

I learned to make this deliciously simple stew, *cap cay*, from Mini, an amazing cook from the mountainous rainforest of Bali. It is a traditional Indonesian dish, and I can see why it's so popular throughout the country. Brimming with a rainbow of healthy veg, the stew is packed with nourishment. Unlike curries or other saucy, spicy stews, *cap cay* is light and clean in flavor. The veggies and their distinct textures, flavors, and colors take center stage, unmasked by a thicker sauce.

My kids love to help cook this soup—and there are plenty of veggies to chop! My boy, Otis, at 10 years old, made *cap cay* for the whole family all by himself.

You can easily make a bowl (or many) in less than an hour, and the recipe is extremely flexible. I encourage you to use a mix of whatever veggies you have in abundance. If you are vegetarian, use tofu in place of the chicken.

Tip: In Bali, *cap cay* is served with a bowl of white rice on the side.

. . . .

serves 4 to 6

¼ cup plus 2 teaspoons coconut oil, divided

1 spicy red or serrano chile pepper, seeded and finely chopped (optional)

1 medium yellow onion, chopped

4 large cloves garlic, pressed or finely chopped

1 pound chicken breast (skin and bones removed), cut into bite-size chunks

Sea salt

4 teaspoons gluten-free tamari

4 cups water

1⅓ cups thinly sliced turnips (slices halved or quartered, depending on size of turnips)

1⅓ cups thinly sliced carrots

4 small tomatoes, diced

8 large button mushrooms, thinly sliced

1⅓ cups corn kernels or sliced baby corn

1⅓ cups sliced green beans

4 shallots, thinly sliced

1 cup raw cashews (you might as well have a few more, just for munching)

2⅔ cups chopped napa cabbage

2⅔ cups chopped bok choy

Set all prepped ingredients near your stove top. It's so helpful to have everything chopped and ready for this very quick-to-cook stew.

Heat a stockpot or large Dutch oven over medium-high heat. Quickly heat ¼ cup of the coconut oil, then turn the heat down to medium. Cook the chile pepper (if using), onion, and garlic in the pot for about 1 minute.

Add the chicken and 1 teaspoon of sea salt. Stir and cook for another minute or so.

Add the tamari and water. Stir and turn the heat to high. When the liquid comes to a boil, add the turnips and carrots. Reduce the heat to a vigorous simmer and cook for 3 minutes.

Add the tomatoes and cook for a minute. Add the mushrooms, corn, and green beans and cook for 2 minutes. Set the stew aside until you're ready to eat.

In a small skillet, cook the shallot over medium-low heat with 1 teaspoon of the remaining coconut oil for 12 to 15 minutes, until golden. Stir the shallot regularly to ensure even cooking. Set aside.

Next, toast the cashews in the remaining 1 teaspoon coconut oil until golden. Set aside.

Just before eating, bring the stew to a simmer. Add the cabbage and bok choy. Stir. Cook only a minute or so, until all the veggies are just tender. Taste for seasoning, and add a little more tamari, if you think it needs it.

Top each serving with plenty of fried shallot and cashews—the tasty toppings are key!

quail with zesty turnips + wilted dandelion greens

We don't eat them often, but quail are a welcome treat at our dinner table any time. Maybe the magic lies in the fact that each tiny quail lends itself to being picked up with your fingers and nibbled. Or maybe it's the mild yet gamey flavor of the tasty birds. Or maybe they are just so easy and quick to cook!

In the early spring, I like to serve the little birds with bitter dandelion greens, cuminy turnips, and a mellow side of creamy polenta. If you want to roast the quail without dandelion or turnips, go for it—quail is a delicious alternative to ubiquitous roast chicken.

serves 4

quail:

4 medium quail, partially deboned
Olive oil
Sea salt
Freshly ground black pepper

turnips + greens:

12 small young snowball turnips, trimmed and quartered, or 1 pound larger turnips, trimmed, peeled, and cut into bite-size pieces

2 tablespoons olive oil
½ teaspoon ground cumin
Zest of 1 lemon
Sea salt
2 bunches (1 pound) dandelion greens, stemmed, and leaves chopped (if you aren't a fan of the bitterness of dandelion greens, kale is a milder alternative)
¼ cup sweetened dried cranberries or sultanas

An hour before you want to cook, take the quail from the fridge. Drizzle on a tablespoon or two of olive oil and season generously with salt and black pepper. Set aside.

When you're ready to cook, preheat the oven to 450°F.

For the turnips and greens: Place the turnips in a roasting pan with the olive oil, cumin, lemon zest, and a generous pinch of salt. Toss to coat. Roast the turnips for 15 to 20 minutes, until tender. Give the roasting pan a shake once or twice during cooking to ensure even browning.

In the meantime, heat a large cast-iron or ovenproof skillet over medium-high heat. When the pan is really hot but not smoking, brown the quail, 3 to 5 minutes per side. You may need to do the browning in a couple of batches depending on the size of your skillet.

Transfer the browned quail in the skillet to the hot oven for 5 to 10 minutes to finish cooking. When the quail are done, the internal temperature should be 145°F degrees and the juices will run clear. (Keep in mind that well-cooked quail can be slightly pinkish on the inside, unlike undercooked chicken.) When the quail are cooked to your liking, let them rest on a plate while you wilt the greens.

Place the chopped greens and cranberries into the skillet in which the quail just finished cooking. Toss to coat with the juices remaining in the pan. Add a pinch of salt and toss the greens again. Return the pan to the hot oven. After 4 to 5 minutes, your greens should be wilted and tender. Toss the roasted turnips with the dandelion greens and cranberries. Season with additional salt to taste.

Serve the roasted quail with wilted greens and zesty turnips.

slow-brew chicken stock

Once you make your own chicken stock, it's hard to imagine returning to the store-bought variety. Paul's simple recipe uses humble chicken scraps instead of an expensive whole bird. Since we are fans of roast chicken, we regularly have the fixings for this simple stock.

After scarfing down a roast chicken dinner, Paul collects all the bones and tosses them in the stockpot, then covers them with water and a few other goodies. Super-slow overnight cooking pulls all the good stuff from the chicken bones and turns tap water into a sumptuous house broth. In the morning, we have a batch of stock to use for soups, stews, and risottos. If we aren't going to use the stock right away, we store it in the freezer until needed.

makes 6 cups

1 whole chicken carcass

1 yellow onion, quartered

2 ribs celery, chopped

2 carrots, chopped

12 black peppercorns

Handful of sprigs fresh flat-leaf
  parsley and/or thyme

1 heaping teaspoon sea salt

14 cups water

Place the chicken carcass, onion, celery, carrots, peppercorns, parsley, and salt in a large stockpot. Pour in the water until the ingredients are fully covered by a couple inches. Partially cover the pot and cook for 10 to 12 hours over the lowest possible heat. You never want this brew to come to a boil (trust me, eventually it will reach a gentle simmer).

After 10 to 12 hours of gentle simmering, turn off the heat and let the stock cool to room temperature. Strain out the solids with a fine-mesh strainer, then place your stock in the fridge. Once the liquid has chilled, scrape off any fat that forms on the top.

Your stock is ready to use.

grain + seed

black rice pudding

Before we moved to Bali for six months, our friends who had already spent time there urged us to learn to make the island's famous black rice pudding. In Bali, this deep purply black porridge—which happens to be rich in antioxidants—graces nearly every menu, and I love that you can eat it for breakfast, at teatime, or as a not-too-sweet dessert. I can see why this exotic comfort food brings on such nostalgia for those who've tried it.

It may not be traditional to top black rice pudding with toasted coconut, but I really like the additional texture it brings to the dish.

Tip: Instead of giving you universal instructions for cooking black rice, I suggest following the directions on the package of rice you buy.

serves 4 to 6

4 cups cooked black rice, not to be confused with long-grain wild rice (1⅓ cups uncooked rice should yield 4 cups cooked)

¼ cup unsweetened flaked coconut

1 vanilla pod or 1 teaspoon vanilla paste

Pinch of sea salt

⅓–½ cup coconut sugar or loosely packed light brown sugar

¼ cup canned coconut milk or coconut cream

Vanilla ice cream (optional)

Preheat the oven to 350°F. Toast the coconut on a baking sheet in the oven for 2 to 3 minutes, until golden. (The coconut burns easily, so keep your eye on it.)

When the rice has cooked, drain out any excess cooking liquid. Use a spoon to scrape out the inside of the vanilla pod (or add the vanilla paste) into the warm rice. Add the salt, sugar, and coconut milk to the pot. (Use more or less sugar, depending on how sweet you like your pudding.) Stir, and your black rice will be glistening and ready to eat. Top with the toasted coconut and splash of coconut milk. Add ice cream, if you like.

golden millet crepes, sweet or savory

I started making millet crepes when we spent a month living on New Zealand's South Island. Cooking in a rented cottage in a foreign country, without the conveniences of our Bay Area markets, forced me to stretch my creative cooking muscles. We were thrilled to find an adorable health food store that sold all sorts of whole grains and seeds. I bought a paper bag full of millet and whipped up some darned tasty crepes. My whole family was happy.

If you are new to crepe making, you'll be amazed at how easy and delicious these are. Please be a bit patient with yourself, as the first few crepes may be a little tricky while you get the hang of the pan and batter. Once you get a rhythm going, you will be flipping millet crepes like a pro.

We like these crepes with both sweet and savory fillings. Sometimes when we invite friends for brunch, I'll set out an array of goodies, make a big stack of crepes, and let everyone stuff them with whatever strikes his or her fancy. Roasted mushrooms and herbed goat cheese is always a great combo, and my Massaged Kale Salad with Dried Cranberries, Pistachios, and Kumquats (page 47) makes a surprisingly tasty filling. On the sweet side, these crepes are amazing with Strawberry Rhubarb Compote with Sprigs of Lemon Thyme (page 220) and a big dollop of Greek yogurt. Or how about a spoonful of Donna's Apricot Jam with Garden Rosemary (page 213) and a smear of butter?

makes 12 (6") crepes

½ cup hulled millet seeds

¾ cup milk (dairy-free friends: unsweetened almond milk or coconut milk is a good substitution here), divided

1 egg

1 tablespoon unsalted butter, softened

Pinch of salt

2 teaspoons maple syrup (optional for sweet crepes)

In a fine-mesh strainer, thoroughly rinse the millet under cool tap water. (Keep in mind that any water left clinging to the seeds after rinsing will help the millet blend with the milk in the next step.)

Place the millet in a standing blender with ¼ cup of the milk. Blend on high for 1 minute, or until you have a thick slurry of ground millet. Use a spatula to scrape down the sides of the blender. Add the remaining ½ cup milk, the egg, softened butter, and salt (also add the 2 teaspoons maple syrup, if you're making sweeter crepes). Blend again on high speed for another 2 minutes, or until your batter is nice and smooth. The batter will be very loose, and that's just right. (At this point, I pour my batter into a mason jar.) Let the batter rest, covered, for 30 minutes, or refrigerate overnight or for up to 2 days before cooking.

When you're ready to cook, heat a small (6" or 7") cast-iron or nonstick skillet over medium heat. (Make sure to give your pan plenty of time to preheat—a hot pan is key to crepes not sticking.) Adjust the heat to ensure your pan is nice and hot but not smoking. Melt a nub of butter to coat the pan. Use a paper towel to rub it around.

Give your batter a good stir (or shake, if it's in a lidded mason jar). Pour 2 tablespoons batter into the hot pan. Immediately lift the pan and give it a quick tilt and swirl, until the batter has evenly coated the bottom of the pan. Cook the crepe for about 1 minute, or until the underside is golden and easily lifts from the pan. Use a butter knife to lift up the edge of the crepe, and flip. Cook the second side for 45 seconds to 1 minute, until your crepe is cooked and speckled with golden bits.

Give the batter a good stir before you make each new crepe, and adjust the heat of the stove as necessary. Using a hot well-seasoned pan, I don't always add more butter for each new crepe, but if you like that extra buttery bite, go for it.

If you have any leftover batter, store it in a lidded container in the fridge for up to 2 days.

best granola ever

I know it's obnoxious to be so boastful about this granola recipe, but really, I'm so damned proud, I can't help myself.

I loved the days my mom made granola when I was growing up. The entire kitchen was warm and toasty and smelled of baked goodness. I couldn't wait to nibble on the chewy clusters. Sadly, Mom's precious granola recipe was lost during her move to Bolinas six years ago. Determined to bring back Mom's granola, I made countless batches before I re-created the flavors, and I'm thrilled to share this recipe with all of you.

I have a few dear friends who regularly make this granola for their families. My heart swells at the idea of a new generation growing up with fond memories of their own warm and toasty kitchens on the days that Mom (or Dad) baked granola.

Of course, you can eat a bowl of granola with milk or yogurt, but it's also good enough to munch on as a snack all by itself. When we go camping, we love to take a batch or two in large jars. We serve it with Greek yogurt and a big fruit salad, making a satisfying breakfast out in the woods by an early morning campfire.

makes 8 cups

2½ cups oats {GF folks: make sure your oats are certified gluten-free}

½ cup sesame seeds

½ cup almond slivers

½ cup sunflower seeds

½ cup sweetened dried cranberries

½ cup unsweetened flaked or shredded coconut

½ cup all-purpose flour {GF folks: use quinoa flour or gluten-free all-purpose flour; see page xxi in "Stocking the Pantry" for suggestions}

½ cup dry milk powder (available in the supermarket baking section)

4 tablespoons unsalted butter, melted

2 tablespoons coconut oil, melted

2 tablespoons olive oil

⅔ cup honey, melted

A couple of pinches nice sea salt (as usual, I like to use Maldon)

Preheat the oven to 275°F.

In a large bowl, mix all ingredients until well integrated. I actually like to do the mixing with my hands, so feel free, if you are so inclined.

Pour the granola onto a large baking sheet. Don't spread it out too much. Keep the granola clumped together near the center of the pan. (I put my oven rack close to the top of the oven so that the bottom doesn't brown too quickly.) Bake for 20 minutes.

Take the granola from the oven, mix, and spread everything out more evenly over the entire baking sheet. Be careful not to break up the clumps too much—we will want those chewy clusters later.

Return to the oven and bake for 8 to 10 minutes. Mix the granola again to ensure even browning.

Finally, bake for 8 to 10 minutes more, and the granola will be ready. At this point, it should be only golden brown and just cooked through, not too dark.

Try to wait until your granola has cooled before indulging in a bowl. As the granola cools, it will firm up and its wonderful texture will emerge, forming irresistible clusters.

Store in an airtight container to maintain the crispy-chewy texture. Honestly, I'm not sure how long granola will keep when stored this way. Ours always gets scarfed up within a few days.

If you are willing to part with a little of this yummy treat, pack up a jar or two to share with friends.

buckwheat zucchini muffins

Believe it or not, buckwheat is not wheat, nor is it even a glutinous cousin of wheat. This sandy-looking grain is actually a relative of sorrel and rhubarb, which is great news for those of us who need to keep gluten out of our kitchens or for anyone looking to explore alternative grains.

These buckwheat muffins are fluffy, incredibly moist, and packed with nutritious ingredients like eggs, oats, grated zucchini, and walnuts, not to mention the fact that buckwheat is packed with protein. The recipe is dairy-free as well. A truly healthy treat!

makes 12

⅔ cup 100% buckwheat flour

½ cup oat flour {GF folks: make sure your oat flour is certified gluten-free}

¾ teaspoon kosher salt

1 teaspoon baking powder

¼ teaspoon baking soda

½ teaspoon ground cinnamon

2 eggs, at room temperature

⅔ cup honey, melted and cooled

⅓ cup coconut oil, melted and cooled

2 tablespoons molasses

1 teaspoon vanilla extract

1¼ cups packed shredded zucchini, patted dry with a paper towel

⅔ cup chopped walnuts

Preheat the oven to 350°F. Line a 12-cup standard muffin pan with paper muffin cups. Sift together the buckwheat flour, oat flour, salt, baking powder, baking soda, and cinnamon in a small bowl.

In a standing mixer with the paddle attachment, or using a large bowl and hand mixer, whisk the eggs. Add the honey, coconut oil, molasses, and vanilla. Mix to blend. Slowly pour in the dry ingredients as you continue mixing. Finally, stir in the zucchini and walnuts.

Pour your batter into the lined cups, using all the batter to fill them. Bake 22 to 25 minutes. You'll know the muffins are done when the top centers are cooked through and no longer sticky to the touch. Cool on a rack.

I particularly like these muffins with a smear of cream cheese on top.

millet porridge

Many of us like a warm grain bowl in the morning, and this millet is a refreshing alternative to omnipresent oatmeal. High in iron and B vitamins, millet porridge can be enjoyed year-round with a huge variety of delicious toppings. In summer, top it with fresh apricots, raspberries, and toasted pistachios. In winter, add roasted apples, or a swirl of jam, almonds, and a splash of cream. You can also add a scoop of Strawberry Rhubarb Compote (page 220), toasted hazelnuts, and a dollop of Greek yogurt.

serves 4

1 cup hulled millet seeds

3 cups water

1 cup milk (cow's, almond, or coconut)

2 tablespoons maple syrup, plus more for serving

Pinch of sea salt

1 cup sliced apricot or pear

1 cup fresh raspberries or chopped pitted cherries

½ cup coarsely chopped roasted salted pistachios or pecans

Small pitcher of heavy cream, for serving

In a fine-mesh strainer, rinse the millet thoroughly under cool tap water.

In a medium saucepan, dry and lightly toast the millet over medium-high heat for 4 minutes, stirring regularly until the seeds become aromatic. Add the water, milk, maple syrup, and a generous pinch of sea salt to the pan. Bring to a boil. Cover and reduce the heat to low. Simmer gently for 30 minutes, or until the millet is tender.

Scoop the porridge into small bowls. Top the millet with sliced apricot, raspberries, pistachios, and a drizzle of heavy cream. Eat right away.

aunt nita's amazing oatmeal cookies

I first tasted these incredible cookies right after our Lilah was born, when my dear friend Eurydice brought over a batch (and a huge glass container full of extra dough). Any moms out there know just how precious food is after you've birthed a baby. Your senses are heightened, and any good bite you take during those first few days after labor are forever remembered with deep appreciation.

I'm not the only one in my house who loves these chewy oatmeal-coconut-walnut gems from Eurydice's Aunt Nita. Every time we make these cookies, everyone in my family chants "Ooooooh Aunt Nita!" and does a happy dance around the kitchen.

Tip: I cannot emphasize enough how important it is to use turbinado sugar in this recipe—the wonderful crunch of coarse raw sugar crystals is key to the magical texture of the cookies.

makes about 36

1 cup (2 sticks) salted butter, softened

1½ cups turbinado sugar

2 eggs, at room temperature

2 teaspoons vanilla extract

2 cups all-purpose flour {GF folks: see page xxi in "Stocking the Pantry" for suggestions}

1 teaspoon baking powder

1 teaspoon baking soda

1 teaspoon kosher salt

1½ cups oats {GF folks: be sure your oats are certified gluten-free}

1½ cups unsweetened flaked coconut

1 cup chopped walnuts

Preheat the oven to 375°F. Grease a baking sheet.

In a standing mixer with the paddle attachment, or in a large bowl with an electric hand mixer, cream the butter and sugar. (Start mixing slowly so the sugar doesn't fly from the bowl.) After mixing, let the creamed butter and sugar sit for 10 minutes.

Add the eggs and vanilla to the butter mixture. Mix to incorporate the ingredients.

In a small bowl, whisk the flour, baking powder, baking soda, and salt. Slowly add the dry ingredients to the wet ingredients, stirring to gently incorporate. Fold in the oats, coconut, and walnuts.

Scoop little mounds of batter onto the greased baking sheet (try to get 36, but don't sweat it if you get more or less). Bake on the upper rack of your oven for 9 to 12 minutes depending on the size of the mounds, only until light and golden. Let the cookies cool on a rack before munching.

polenta fries

Crispy on the outside, fluffy and tender on the inside, these polenta fries can be enjoyed in so many ways. Serve them for dipping into soup or a steaming bowl of mussels, or with poached eggs or warm beans. By cutting the polenta into smaller squares before baking, you can quickly transform the fries into croutons and scatter them onto a big salad. You get the picture—these tasty guys are versatile and damned good.

Tip: I use instant polenta in this recipe to keep the prep easier, but if you've got time on your hands, feel free to use slow-cooking polenta.

serves 6 to 8

Sea salt

1 cup instant polenta

3 tablespoons unsalted butter

1 cup grated Parmesan

Plenty of freshly ground black pepper

Bring 3½ cups water, with a generous pinch of sea salt, to a boil in a large heavy-bottom saucepan. Once you have a rolling boil, slowly pour the polenta into the water while whisking continuously. Turn the heat down to medium-high and continue whisking for 2 to 3 minutes, until the polenta has thickened and is cooked through. Stir in the butter and ¾ cup of the Parmesan. Season with ample freshly ground black pepper and plenty of sea salt to taste.

Transfer the warm polenta to an 11" x 7" baking dish. Using the back of a wooden spoon or spatula, smooth the polenta into an even layer. Let the polenta cool and firm up in your fridge for at least 45 minutes.

Preheat the oven to 450°F. Line one or two baking sheets with parchment paper.

Cut the polenta into 2½" x ½" (finger-size) strips. (If you want to make croutons, cut the strips into smaller squares.) Place the polenta strips/cubes onto the baking sheet(s). Don't overcrowd the strips—they need some room to brown on the sides. Slide the baking sheet(s) into the oven. After 10 minutes, flip the fries, sprinkle on the remaining ¼ cup Parmesan, return to the oven, and bake for 10 minutes. Serve hot.

If you have any leftover fries, toast them up in the oven the next day for breakfast.

parmesan polenta with garlicky rapini and black olives

Preparing a proper polenta does take some time, but that old myth of it needing constant stirring is just not true. For this simple supper, allow yourself an hour of very low-key cooking, during which you can relax, chat with your family, or sneak a read while the simmering cornmeal mostly takes care of itself.

Creamy polenta, spicy greens, and briny olives make a feisty one-bowl vegetarian meal, but I also encourage you to make this polenta to accompany a myriad of goodies beyond rapini, like roasted wild mushrooms, sausages, all sorts of sautéed greens, Pork Ragù with Candied Tomatoes (page 133), or Bourbon-Braised Short Ribs with Brown Sugar and Coffee (page 131). You can even make a batch of polenta with garlicky greens for brunch and top it with poached eggs.

serves 4

polenta:

4½ cups water

Sea salt

1 cup polenta (not the instant variety)

Whole milk, as needed, or additional
    water

4–6 tablespoons unsalted butter

¾ cup grated Parmesan

rapini:

2 large bunches rapini

¼ cup olive oil

5 cloves garlic, thinly slivered

Sea salt

¼ cup pitted and chopped wrinkly,
    oil-cured black olives

¼–½ teaspoon red-pepper flakes
    (optional)

First, make your polenta: Heat the water (with ½ teaspoon sea salt) in a medium, heavy-bottom saucepan over high heat. When the water comes to a rolling boil, slowly pour in the polenta, whisking continuously and vigorously for 1 to 2 minutes, until the polenta has made friends with the water and has thickened into one nice brew. Reduce the heat to low in order achieve a whisper of a simmer.

Let the polenta gently cook, uncovered, for 50 minutes, stirring only every 10 minutes. (Feel free to occasionally add splashes of milk if your polenta gets too thick.) After 50 minutes, stir in the butter, another splash of milk, and ½ cup

of the Parmesan. Taste for seasoning and add more salt as needed. Let the polenta rest covered, off the heat, for 10 minutes before serving.

While your polenta is resting, prepare the rapini: Trim an inch off the woody end of each rapini stalk. Then coarsely chop all remaining stems, leaves and florets—remember, all parts are tasty when cooked. You need about 8 cups. In a large skillet, heat the olive oil over medium heat. Add the garlic slivers to the warm oil and add the chopped rapini immediately, along with a pinch of sea salt. Toss to coat the greens, then cover the pan and turn the heat down to medium-low. Cook covered for 8 to 12 minutes, until tender, then add the olives and red-pepper flakes, if you like the spice, to the greens. Season with additional sea salt, if you think it needs it.

Serve the creamy polenta in shallow bowls topped with a huge pile of sautéed rapini and its zesty compatriots. Scatter the remaining ¼ cup Parmesan over the top of each dish.

If you have leftovers, scoop them into an ovenproof dish covered with aluminum foil and refrigerate. Rewarm in a 350°F oven for 20 minutes.

spaghetti dinner with rainbow chard, bacon, and cream

This decadent recipe is the result of a desperate need to toss together a quick family supper without wanting to take a trip to the market. Using leftovers, pantry goodies, and a bushel of fresh greens, we ended up with a meal our entire family loves and has since been on frequent rotation at our house. Who knew that clearing out the fridge could taste so good?

serves 4

Sea salt

2 large bunches rainbow chard

2 tablespoons olive oil

½ pound bacon

1 package dried spaghetti {GF folks: see page xxi in "Stocking the Pantry" for suggestions}

⅓ cup heavy cream

½ cup finely grated Parmesan, plus ¼–½ cup for serving

Plenty of freshly ground black pepper

Put a large pot of pasta water on to boil. Add salt generously until it tastes like seawater.

Remove the stems from the chard. Thinly slice the stems and set aside. Cut the leaves into a rough chiffonade.

Heat a large skillet over medium heat. Add the olive oil. Toss in the chopped chard stems and a pinch of sea salt. Cover and cook until the stems are barely tender. Add the leaves and toss them with the stems. Cover again and continue to cook until the greens are tender as well. Drain any excess cooking water from the greens and set aside in a bowl.

Give your large skillet a quick wash and place it back on the stove top over medium heat. Cut the bacon horizontally into matchstick-size strips and place them in the hot pan. Let your bacon strips get nice and crisp (about 10 minutes of cooking). Flip as needed during cooking to ensure even crisping.

After the bacon has been sizzling for 5 minutes, start cooking the pasta. {I suggest stirring GF pasta at the beginning of cooking to ensure that the strands don't stick together.} When the pasta is done, drain and set it aside—though hopefully your timing will coincide perfectly with the sauce's completion.

When the bacon is crispy, turn off the heat. Pour out excess bacon grease, leaving a tablespoon or so in the pan to mix in with the sauce. (Decadent, I know!) Add cream to the bacon and whisk to loosen those bacon bits still clinging to the pan. Then add the cooked chard to the creamy bacon party. Toss to coat. Finally, add the pasta and ½ cup of the Parmesan to the pan. Toss. Generously grind black pepper over the pasta. Season with salt to taste.

Serve immediately and pass around the pepper mill and a bowl of extra Parmesan.

I love that the chard is tender, the sauce is creamy, and the bacon is crispy. Perfect!

red rice risotto with wild mushrooms and wilted spinach

While I am a sucker for traditional risottos, I feel no need to limit this fabulous cooking method to white rice. We discovered the deliciousness of red rice when we lived in Bali—it's hearty like farro or barley, without the gluten. Red rice risotto is not quite as creamy as your traditional risotto, but the nutty bite is unexpected and tastes of nourishment. The earthy grain is delectable paired with wild mushrooms and tender spinach. In the wintertime, this is the kind of healthy comfort food I want to scoop from a bowl as I cozy up to a warm fire.

If you use veggie stock, red rice risotto makes a great vegetarian main course. If you are a meat eater, you can serve it with a simple roast chicken and leafy salad, or with some spicy chicories on the side.

If you are anything like me and enjoy the visual pleasure of cooking as well as the smells and tastes, I think you will love the colors at work here. The red rice, shallots, rosé, and chanterelles make for a gorgeous, rosy palette to cook from.

serves 3 or 4 as a main, or 6 to 8 as a side

1½ cups Bhutanese red rice (short- or medium-grain brown rice works here too)

3 cups boiling water

3 tablespoons olive oil, divided

4 cups fresh chanterelle or hedgehog mushrooms, chopped

2 cloves garlic, minced

2 tablespoons fresh thyme leaves or a few sprigs

Sea salt

Freshly ground black pepper

5 cups chicken or veggie stock (page 148 or 90)

3 tablespoons unsalted butter, divided

⅓ cup finely chopped shallot

¼ cup dry rosé or white wine

4 cups packed spinach leaves

¾ cup grated Parmesan, plus more for serving

Place your rice in a medium bowl, and pour the boiling hot water over it. Let it soak while you prep your other ingredients.

Over medium heat, warm 2 tablespoons of the olive oil in a large skillet. Toss in the mushrooms, garlic, thyme, a sprinkling of sea salt, and a few grinds of black pepper. Cook until the mushrooms are tender and have released their

liquid. Set the cooked mushrooms aside, pouring off any excess cooking liquid.

In a large saucepan on the back burner of your stove, heat the stock. Adjust the heat to keep the broth heated at just below a simmer throughout the cooking process.

Just before cooking the risotto, drain the rice. Save the soaking liquid and pour it into the pan of warm broth.

In a large heavy-bottom stockpot or Dutch oven, heat the remaining 1 tablespoon olive oil and 1 tablespoon of the butter over medium heat. When the butter is bubbling, add the shallot and cook for 1 to 2 minutes, until it becomes slightly translucent but not at all browned. Next, add the rice and stir to coat grains with the warm fats. After 2 minutes, add the wine to the pot and cook for a minute or two, until most of the wine has been absorbed or evaporated. Next, add a ladleful of warm broth to the rice. Let the rice cook and absorb most of the liquid. Then add enough broth to lightly cover the rice and adjust the stove heat to keep a hearty simmer going. Stir regularly, and keep adding ladlefuls of broth every few minutes to ensure that the rice is always cooking under a thin layer of broth.

Continue cooking your risotto for a total of 30 to 40 minutes, or until the rice is plump and cooked through, but still has a toothsome quality. When the risotto tastes done to you, turn the heat to low, stir in the mushrooms, spinach leaves, and one last ladleful of broth. Season with salt generously to taste. Cover the pot for just a couple minutes, allowing the spinach to wilt. Once the spinach has wilted, turn off the heat completely and stir in the remaining 2 tablespoons butter, the Parmesan, plus a little more salt and pepper to taste. Cover the pot again and let the flavors come together for 5 minutes before serving. Serve with additional grated Parmesan.

Tip: If you have leftovers, pop them in the fridge—the risotto can be enjoyed for days and the flavors will only deepen. Reheat leftover risotto in a covered baking dish in a 350°F oven.

pip's yellow rice

You will find a version of yellow rice, *nasi kuning*, at nearly every restaurant in Indonesia. Turmeric, a powerful anti-inflammatory, is the magic behind the signature color. The regal golden hue is said to bring good fortune, which is always a good thing in my book.

Our talented chef buddy Pip kindly shared his version of yellow rice with us. I like that Pip adds golden aromatics to cooked rice through a quick spice-infused butter. This dish is packed with flavor while still being easy to make. Just be forewarned that if you are new to using turmeric, it really can stain your fingers, cutting boards, and so on. The stuff is powerful indeed.

Serve with grilled fish or chicken, or I especially love yellow rice with Prawns on Lemongrass Skewers (page 112) for a taste of Indonesia.

Tip: Look for fresh lemongrass stalks and turmeric root in your local Asian market.

serves 4

1 cup basmati or jasmine rice

Sea salt

3 tablespoons unsalted butter

2 small or 1 medium shallot, finely chopped

2 tablespoons grated fresh turmeric root, if you can get it; otherwise, use 1 teaspoon ground turmeric

1½ tablespoons grated fresh ginger

3 lemongrass stalks, light tender ends finely chopped for a total of 3 tablespoons

3 cloves garlic, minced

3 tablespoons canned light coconut milk

¼ cup chopped fresh cilantro leaves (optional)

Lime wedges, for serving (optional)

In a fine-mesh strainer, rinse the rice under cool tap water. Place in a medium saucepan with 1½ cups water and a pinch of sea salt, cover, and turn the heat to high. Once the water is boiling and the lid rattling, turn the heat down to low, allowing the rice to cook at a gentle simmer. After 15 minutes, remove the pan from the heat and let it sit, covered, for 10 minutes.

While the rice is cooking, melt the butter in a small saucepan over medium heat and cook the shallot in the butter for 5 minutes, or until golden. Next, add the turmeric, ginger, lemongrass, garlic, and a pinch of salt. Continue to cook, stirring regularly for 4 minutes, until all the spices and butter have become good friends.

Fluff the cooked rice with a fork, then fold the buttery spices into the rice. Season generously with salt to taste. Add the coconut milk and stir again. Top with the cilantro leaves, if desired. Serve with lime wedges if you want to squeeze them over the golden rice.

diy corn tortillas

There is something undeniably playful about making your own corn tortillas. Years ago, we bought a metal tortilla press at a Mexican market, and I'm so glad we did. My kids get pumped up and ready to help whenever it's tortilla-making time. If you've got eager little hands in your kitchen, get those kiddos involved with every step of the process. Making tortillas is fun and super tactile, from hand-mixing the dough to rolling balls to pressing tortillas. All good stuff!

When making tortillas yourself, you get to decide what size to make 'em. A standard tortilla press can accommodate a 6" tortilla, but we've fallen in love with making mini rounds. You can also customize the thickness of your tortillas, depending on your preference. If you like your tortillas thin, just use a little extra muscle when you squish the dough.

makes 24 (3½") or 12 (6") tortillas

2 cups masa harina {GF folks: check your labels}

½ teaspoon kosher salt

1–1½ cups warm tap water

In a medium bowl, mix the masa harina, salt, and water with your hands. You want your dough to be moist and pliable, yet not soggy with wetness. Add a bit more water or masa harina to have a nice consistency. Cover with a clean, damp kitchen towel and let rest at room temperature for 1 hour.

Use your hands to roll balls of dough—think of those days spent rolling clay between your palms in elementary school. For mini tortillas, you want the balls to be about the size of a very small tangerine (2" in diameter). Make them larger—just over 3"—if you want larger tortillas. Once you are done forming the balls of dough, get out your tortilla press.

Line the tortilla press with 2 squares of parchment paper. Press one ball of dough at a time. Set the tortillas aside.

Heat a large nonstick skillet or griddle over medium-high heat. Cook each tortilla for 1 to 2 minutes per side, until golden. I keep my cooked tortillas warm in a ceramic dish lined with a cloth napkin or two. Serve warm.

rainbow quinoa with curried chickpeas, crispy kale, apple, and fennel

This salad has a whole slew of flavors and textures going for it, and each bite highlights a different element—a whisper of curry here, the sweet crunch of apple there, an airy bite of crispy kale there. As you're preparing components of the salad, it may feel daunting, but once you toss everything together your hard work will pay off. This is the kind of nourishing one-bowl meal that makes me seriously consider giving up my carnivorous ways.

serves 2 or 3 as a main, or 4 to 6 as a side

quinoa:

½ cup quinoa (I use rainbow quinoa, but any quinoa will do)

1 teaspoon olive oil

Sea salt

crispy kale:

4 cups tightly packed kale leaves, stems removed, fully dried

1 tablespoon olive oil

Sea salt

curried chickpeas:

1 teaspoon olive oil or coconut oil

1 teaspoon curry powder

1 small shallot, thinly sliced

1 cup cooked chickpeas, rinsed and drained

Sea salt

other goodies:

1 small bulb fennel, sliced paper-thin (discard tough core)

1 Fuji apple, very thinly sliced, then slices halved

1 teaspoon red wine vinegar

1 tablespoon extra-virgin olive oil

Zest and juice of 1 lemon

Sea salt

For the quinoa: Soak the quinoa for 15 minutes in 1 cup cool tap water. Using a fine-mesh strainer, vigorously rinse the quinoa under cold running water to wash off any bitterness.

Preheat the oven to 350°F for the kale.

Heat the olive oil in a small saucepan over medium heat. When hot, add your quinoa and toast, stirring occasionally, for 5 minutes. Add 1 cup water

and a pinch of sea salt to the saucepan. Turn up the heat to high. Once the liquid is boiling, cover the pan and reduce the heat to achieve a nice simmer. Cook the quinoa until tender, 15 to 18 minutes. Let the quinoa sit covered, off the heat, for 10 minutes before mixing with the other salad ingredients.

While your quinoa is cooking, go ahead and make the crispy kale. Coarsely chop the leaves into bite-size pieces and scatter them onto a large baking sheet. Drizzle the olive oil over the leaves. Use your hands to toss the leaves to coat with the oil, and sprinkle with sea salt. Crisp the kale in the oven for 10 to 12 minutes.

Quickly make the curried chickpeas while the quinoa and kale are cooking. Heat the oil in a small skillet over medium heat. Add the curry powder and shallot to the pan. Let sizzle for 2 to 3 minutes, then add the chickpeas. Toss to coat. Continue cooking for 3 to 4 minutes. Season generously with salt to taste.

Finally, it's time to assemble the salad. Get out a large salad bowl, and combine the warm quinoa with the curried chickpeas, crispy kale, fennel, and apple pieces. Give everything a good toss with your hands. Don't worry if the kale crumbles into the salad—that's what you want. Season the salad with the splash of red wine vinegar, a drizzle of olive oil, and the lemon zest and juice. Season again with sea salt to taste.

Eat right away.

popped amaranth with cumin, coriander, and sesame seeds

Popped amaranth is a quick and healthy snack. The tiny seeds are inexpensive and packed with protein and calcium, and prepping takes less than 5 minutes. Popping amaranth is messy, so if you've got kids, get them involved with making this wholesome treat and don't worry if some amaranth leaps out of the pan as it's popping—the spontaneous confetti is part of the fun.

I credit my middle-schooler, Otis, for introducing amaranth to our kitchen. He is a lucky kid attending King Middle School—the home of Alice Waters's original Edible Schoolyard—and he comes home gushing about new recipes for us to try. At the Edible Schoolyard, not only do the kids cook amaranth, but they grow and harvest it as well. Otis loves the ESY recipe for faux "Rice Crispy" treats made with popped amaranth and brown rice syrup.

I wanted to take my popped amaranth in a savory direction and was deeply influenced by the flavors found in dukkah, a wonderful Middle Eastern spice blend. You can nibble on this spiced popped amaranth as a great snack on its own, or feel free to scatter some onto a bowl of soup, or a platter of sautéed greens, or over the top of a salad.

You can also treat naked popped amaranth as a light breakfast cereal.

Tip: Be a little patient with yourself if you are new to popping amaranth. Mastering this simple technique can take a few attempts, but once you get the hang of it, you'll be popping up a storm.

....

makes 3 to 4 cups

½ cup raw amaranth

¼ cup raw sesame seeds

2 teaspoons olive oil

½ teaspoon ground cumin

¼ teaspoon ground coriander

Sea salt

In a small bowl, stir together the amaranth and sesame seeds. Place the bowl, along with a tablespoon-size measuring spoon, next to the stove. Also place a baking sheet next to the stove to hold the seeds once they've popped.

Heat a deep, heavy-bottom saucepan over high heat. When the pan is nice and hot but not smoking, add a sprinkle of water. If the water beads and scampers across the surface, you are ready to pop your seeds. Wipe out the water and pour 2 tablespoons of the amaranth-sesame mix into the hot dry pot. Stir immediately and continuously with a spoon and watch the golden amaranth quickly pop into tiny white kernels (don't worry about the sesame seeds . . . they don't need to pop like the amaranth to taste good). Amaranth burns easily, so keep stirring vigorously and remove the pan from the heat as soon as the majority of amaranth has popped. The whole process will take less than 30 seconds!

Pour the popped seeds onto the waiting baking sheet. Repeat the process of popping the seeds in small batches and transferring them to the baking sheet until you're all done.

Drizzle the olive oil over your popped amaranth and sesame. Sprinkle with the cumin, coriander, and sea salt to your liking. Toss with your hands.

Store popped amaranth at room temperature in a lidded container and enjoy within a week.

quinoa tabbouleh with tomatoes, scallions, parsley leaves, and blossoms

I've been making this recipe for years and find it so satisfying in the late summer, when tomatoes are at their peak of sweet abundance. When the weather is warm, the last thing anyone wants for dinner is a hot meal. This quinoa is filling while still being light, refreshing, and full of herby, lemony zing. It's easy to forget that traditional tabbouleh is made with bulgur—quinoa is so good here that it feels made for this Mediterranean classic.

This is one of my favorite dishes to bring to a picnic or potluck. And leftovers are delicious, if you have any!

This dish is best made at least an hour ahead of time so all the flavors can mingle and the quinoa can soak up all the goodness.

serves 6 to 8

1½ cups quinoa

½ teaspoon kosher salt

3 cups chopped tomatoes (bite-size pieces)

1½ cups finely chopped fresh flat-leaf parsley

¼–½ cup finely chopped scallions

¼–⅓ cup freshly squeezed lemon juice

½ cup extra-virgin olive oil

2 tablespoons finely chopped fresh mint leaves

Flaky sea salt (Maldon is my favorite)

Parsley blossoms, for garnish (optional)

First, rinse the quinoa thoroughly in a fine-mesh strainer under running tap water. Place the rinsed quinoa in a large saucepan with 3 cups of water and let the grains soak for at least 15 minutes. Bring to a boil. Add the kosher salt to the pot. Reduce the heat, cover, and simmer until the water is absorbed and the quinoa is fluffy and tender, 15 to 17 minutes. Let cool to room temperature.

In a large bowl, toss the quinoa with the tomatoes, parsley, scallions, lemon juice, olive oil, and mint. Add salt and additional lemon juice to your liking, and you've got your tabbouleh.

Serve the quinoa at room temp. Feel free to add a little more flaky sea salt and an extra drizzle of nice olive oil at serving time, and top with the blossoms, if you have 'em.

mixed grains with asparagus, favas, watercress, and toasted pine nuts

This risotto-like dish is packed with spring vegetables, which make delectable companions to simply cooked millet, quinoa, and amaranth. A verdant puree of watercress, lemon, olive oil, and garlic coats the grains, and salty pecorino brings a creaminess to the whole venture. A sprinkling of fresh watercress leaves and toasted pine nuts finishes with a little crunch. A luscious one-bowl vegetarian meal—this is my kind of lunch.

I've used a mix of grains in order to broaden our horizons, but keep in mind that you could use quinoa on its own, or even brown rice would be delicious. And if favas are hard to find, you can skip them altogether, or substitute with English or snow peas, and the dish will still taste great.

Tip: Shucking favas should be a communal event to be enjoyed. Call everyone to the back stoop or kitchen table and get all those hands working. After you shuck and blanch your favas, you'll need to release the tender beans from their rubbery husks. To do so, pinch a hole in one side and gingerly squeeze the pod between your fingers, and the beans should pop right out.

serves 4 to 6

mixed grains:

½ cup amaranth

½ cup millet

½ cup quinoa

Sea salt

veggies:

Sea salt

2 pounds fresh favas in their pods (English peas or snow peas are nice alternatives)

1 pound asparagus spears, tough ends removed

puree:

2 cups watercress

2 or 3 cloves garlic, finely chopped

¼ cup extra-virgin olive oil

Zest and juice of 1 lemon

Sea salt

toppings:

¾ cup grated pecorino or Parmesan

Sea salt

½ cup watercress leaves

¾–1 cup pine nuts, toasted

As you prep, don't worry if your cooked ingredients cool—the dish can be eaten at any temperature.

For the grains: Place the amaranth, millet, and quinoa in a fine-mesh strainer and rinse thoroughly with tap water. Transfer your rinsed grains to a large saucepan or small stockpot. Cover with 2½ cups fresh tap water and soak the grains for 30 minutes. Place the saucepan over high heat, add a pinch of salt, and bring to a boil. Cover, reduce the heat to low, and simmer for 17 to 20 minutes, until tender.

While the grains are cooking, fill a stockpot with tap water for cooking the veggies. Add a generous amount of salt. Shuck the favas from their pods, as you would shell peas. Blanch the asparagus spears and favas for 2 to 5 minutes (cooking time will depend on the thickness of your asparagus and size of your favas). After 2 minutes, begin testing for doneness: Take an asparagus spear and fava from the pot and taste to see if the veggies are tender and cooked to your liking. Vibrant green, just-tender vegetables are what you're looking for.

Plunge the cooked veg into an ice bath (a medium bowl with water and ice). When your veggies are cool enough to handle, pop the favas from their rubbery skins (discard these skins) to reveal the shiny beans underneath. Drain the asparagus and slice the spears into bite-size pieces.

For the puree: Using a mortar and pestle or a food processor, puree the watercress, garlic, olive oil, lemon zest, and lemon juice. Season with salt to taste.

When the grains are cooked, remove the saucepan from the stove top and let the grains rest in the pot for 5 minutes. Transfer to a large serving bowl or platter. Add the favas and asparagus, pour the green puree over the grains and veggies, and stir to coat. Stir in most of the grated pecorino, then add salt to taste. Top the dish with the watercress leaves, toasted pine nuts, and another dusting of pecorino.

You can keep leftovers in the fridge in a lidded container, and you've got lunch ready to take to work the next day.

nut

toasty pecans with garden rosemary, honey, and smoked salt

Who doesn't crave a good snack, especially when it comes to cocktail time? The smoky, herby, sweet, salty crunch of these pecans seems made for nibbling while sipping a cold drink. {GF folks: Check out my GF beer suggestions on page xxii—there's no need for anyone to be left out.}

Once you've made a batch of these pecans, you'll find they can be put to good use in so many ways beyond the cocktail hour. Serve them alongside fresh figs and crème fraîche for a quick dessert. They also make a tasty addition to Pears with Stilton + Honeycomb (page 235). Or why not toss a handful into your breakfast porridge or a bowl of Greek yogurt with sliced peaches. Ahhhhh, the possibilities. . . .

makes 1½ cups

½ tablespoon unsalted butter

1 generous tablespoon honey

2 tablespoons fresh rosemary leaves

1½ cups raw pecans (6 ounces)

Few pinches smoked sea salt (any nice sea salt will do, but smoked salt is particularly amazing here)

Preheat the oven to 300°F. Line a baking sheet with parchment paper.

In a small saucepan, melt the butter and honey over medium-low heat. When everything is warm and melted, toss in the rosemary leaves and stir to coat. Turn off your burner, cover the pan, and let the honey and butter infuse with herby goodness for 5 minutes. Finally, toss the nuts into the pan and stir to coat. Scatter the sticky pecans onto the baking sheet and put 'em in the oven.

Bake for 13 to 15 minutes, until the pecans are lightly toasted. Immediately sprinkle the smoked salt over the hot pecans. Let them cool fully and firm up before serving.

Store the pecans in an airtight container. If you feel like sharing, you can pack some into little mason jars to give as a hostess gift.

hazelnut meringue clusters

I first tasted hazelnut meringues at a charming Italian gelato shop in Bali . . . talk about globalism. When I saw the name "ugly but good"—which turns out to be a classic Tuscan treat, *brutti ma buoni*—I was charmed by the underdog spirit of these little cookies.

Returning to our Berkeley kitchen, I wanted to make my own version for our family. The cookies are so fun to cook with kids: Watch their eyes bulge as three little egg whites turn into a mountain of marshmallowy deliciousness. The whipped eggy concoction is so tasty that there's always a fight over who gets to lick the spatula clean.*

These sweet, fluffy treats are packed with hazelnuts and have surprisingly little sugar. Plus, they are naturally GF and dairy-free too!

Tip: Save your egg yolks for the Old School Caesar (page 56) or a batch of homemade mayo.

makes 30

1 cup raw hazelnuts

½ lemon

3 egg whites, at room temperature

½ cup superfine sugar (available in the baking section of your market)

Pinch of sea or kosher salt

1 teaspoon vanilla extract

Preheat the oven to 375°F. Line 2 baking sheets with parchment paper for baking the meringues later.

In a small, dry cast iron pan, toast the hazelnuts in the oven for 7 to 10 minutes. Let the nuts cool, then rub off the skins using a clean kitchen towel. Coarsely crush the hazelnuts with a mortar and pestle, or use a heavy chef's knife. Set the nuts aside, and turn the oven down to 350°F.

Get out a medium bowl and hand mixer, or a standing mixer with the whisk attachment. (It is key to have your bowl and whisk completely grease-free in order to make successful meringues: Rub the lemon half all around the inside of your mixing bowl and on the whisk attachment itself.) Vigorously whisk the egg whites until soft peaks form. While the mixer is still running,

Eat raw eggs at your own discretion.

gradually add the sugar, salt, and vanilla. Continue high-speed whisking for a few more minutes, until the eggs have formed stiff peaks and become beautifully glossy. Gently fold in the crushed hazelnuts.

Scoop small mounds of batter onto the prepared baking sheets. Bake for 15 minutes, then turn off the oven and let the meringues continue to crisp in the warm oven for an hour or so. Store the cookies in an airtight container to preserve crispness.

pistachio pesto with parsley and piave

Three years ago, when I brought my mom home from the hospital after her cancer surgery, I was thrilled when she said she was hungry. "What do you crave, Mom?" I asked. "Pesto, please," she said with hungry eyes. I was honored to cook for my mom, to do anything that could potentially play even a small part in her healing process.

I took a quick trip to the little hippie grocery in her coastal California town. There were no pine nuts to be found, though thankfully there were handsome pistachios calling to me. I zipped back to Mom's and made her a big batch of pistachio pesto, and she wolfed it down. I poured all my love into that pesto, and I like to think it helped her just a bit.

With the price of pine nuts reaching the stratosphere, pistachio pesto has become a staple at our house. Of course, we use pesto to top bowls of spaghetti or Zucchini Ribbon "Pasta" (page 61), and we also happily serve it on poached eggs, baked fish, and roasted pork. I like to stir a spoonful of pesto into a warm bowl of beans, and I've been known to spread it onto my morning toast.

Instead of parsley, go ahead and make this pesto with basil if you prefer, and if you can't find Piave, you'll never go wrong using a really nice aged Parmesan.

Tip: If you're using raw pistachios, do the following: Heat a medium skillet over medium heat on the stove top. Toss in raw pistachios and toast, giving them a shake occasionally to ensure even browning. When you really smell the nuts roasting, after 5 to 7 minutes, take them off the heat. Set the pistachios aside and cool to room temp before using.

makes 1½ cups

½ cup roasted salted pistachios; if you are using raw nuts, see the tip

2 cups loosely packed fresh flat-leaf parsley leaves

¼ cup finely grated Piave (if you cannot find Piave, you can just use Parmesan)

¼ cup finely grated Parmesan, plus more for serving

2 cloves garlic, pressed or finely chopped

Sea salt

Freshly ground black pepper

½–¾ cup olive oil

Place the pistachios, parsley, grated cheeses, garlic, salt, and black pepper in a food processor or blender with just enough of the olive oil to make the mixture move—about ½ cup. (If you have a standard blender as I do, you'll need to get out a spatula to help move around all of the ingredients to blend.) Taste to see if you'd like additional salt or pepper. If you use salted pistachios you won't need to add much extra salt.

Store the pesto in the fridge in a lidded container. Drizzle just enough of the remaining olive oil to cover the top of the pesto to prevent browning. You can also freeze a jar for later use. Or you may want to bring some to a friend in need of comfort food.

simple almond torte with garden strawberries + crème fraîche

Almond flour is a boon to any gluten-free kitchen. It may just be my favorite ingredient when it comes to baking without wheat. This torte shows off the honest deliciousness of almond meal—you get a moist, marzipan-esque treat packed with almondy richness. Plus, this torte is not too sweet and has no refined sugar, making it a good breakfast item or afternoon snack, as well as a more traditional dessert.

The torte can be sliced and eaten it on its own, and it is fantastic as the base of a simple fruit tart. We have a sunny rock wall in our backyard garden dedicated to strawberries of all sorts. These happy little berries, along with a dollop of homemade crème fraîche, make great toppings to the buttery almond crust. You can also serve the torte with crème fraîche and Boozy Cherries with Port, Honey, and Bay (page 239), Strawberry Rhubarb Compote with Sprigs of Lemon Thyme (page 220), or Donna's Apricot Jam with Garden Rosemary (page 213).

serves 4 (makes 1 small torte)

5 tablespoons unsalted butter

1½ cups lightly packed almond meal

1 egg yolk

⅓ cup golden honey

1 teaspoon almond extract

½ teaspoon vanilla extract

Pinch of sea salt

⅓ cup almond slices

½ cup crème fraîche (see page 266 for making your own)

1 basket fresh strawberries, trimmed and sliced

Melt the butter and set it aside to cool for 5 to 10 minutes.

In a medium bowl, combine the melted butter, almond meal, egg yolk, honey, almond extract, vanilla, and salt, and mix until integrated. Your batter will be thick and sticky.

Thoroughly butter a 13" x 4" tart pan or a 7" round pan (with removable bottom). Scoop the batter into the buttered pan and spread to distribute evenly, using your fingers, a rubber spatula, or the back of a wooden spoon. Place the pan in the freezer for 20 minutes to chill.

Preheat the oven to 300°F.

Scatter the almond slices over the top of the tart dough and slide the pan into the oven. Bake for 30 to 35 minutes, until the torte is light golden brown. (Don't overbake—the moistness of the almond meal really shines in a just-cooked torte.) Let cool completely on a rack before serving.

Serve each slice of torte topped with a dollop of crème fraîche and some sliced strawberries.

pistachio tangerine sugar cookies

Pistachios and tangerines are meant for one another. In these simple sugar cookies, the happy union of the two ingredients is the highlight of every bite. Crispy, crunchy, and slightly salty, these cookies are delightful served alongside a cup of tea in the afternoon, or with vanilla ice cream for dessert. Plus, it's always nice to have a roll of cookie dough in the freezer so you can bust out some fresh baked goods for a guest or an impromptu dinner party.

Shelling pistachios is the only laborious part of the recipe. In the evening after dinner, I can usually rope Otis or Lilah into helping me with this task. While we pull pistachios from their shells, we chat about our day and dream about the nutty cookies that await us.

makes 35 to 40

1 cup shelled roasted salted pistachios (10–12 ounces in the shell)

½ cup (1 stick) unsalted butter, softened

¾ cup turbinado sugar

1 egg yolk

⅓ cup quinoa flour or all-purpose flour {GF folks: see page xxi in "Stocking the Pantry" for suggestions}

½ teaspoon tangerine or orange zest

½ teaspoon orange flower water

Maldon or other flaky sea salt

Grind the pistachios in a blender until they are the consistency of cornmeal; a coarse flour-like texture is what you're looking for.

In a standing mixer, or using a hand mixer and large bowl, cream together the butter and sugar. Add the egg yolk. Continue mixing, then add the ground pistachios, flour, zest, orange flower water, and a generous pinch of salt until well blended.

Lay out 2 pieces of plastic wrap and make 2 logs of cookie dough, each about 1" in diameter. Wrap the dough in the plastic and chill the wrapped dough in the freezer for at least half an hour.

Preheat the oven to 300°F. Line 2 baking sheets with parchment paper.

Slice the cookie logs into ¼"-thick rounds and place them onto the baking sheets. (Give the cookies a little room in case they spread a bit while baking.)

If any of your rounds break apart when you're slicing them, just squeeze them back together—all that butter will work its magic.

Bake the cookies for 20 to 22 minutes, until golden brown around the edges. Let the cookies cool on a rack. Wait to eat the cookies until after they have cooled—that's when the irresistible crunchy texture emerges.

These cookies can be kept crisp and ready to eat in a sealed container for a few days.

brown butter almond tea cakes
with nectarine slivers

In the three months we spent traveling throughout Australia and New Zealand, we found the Aussies and Kiwis to be years ahead of the United States in terms of accommodating gluten-free eaters. Every café offered at least one, if not two or three, delectable, gluten-free baked goods, and sometimes the GF options outnumbered their wheaty cousins.

"Friands"—almond tea cakes, and relatives of the French financier—were irresistible as we ate our way through cities like Melbourne, Auckland, and Sydney. Friands have since become a favorite recipe in our baking repertoire. The brown butter richness and slightly caramelized and chewy edges of these almond cakes are a delicious contrast to the moist and fluffy innards. You need not be gluten-free to love friands!

This recipe is a riff on one I stumbled upon in *Donna Hay* magazine during our travels Down Under. I've topped my friands with nectarine slices, but you can also use little bits of whatever seasonal fruit you have around, or even bake the friands without any fruit at all; they can easily hold their own.

Tip: Save your egg yolks for making an Old School Caesar (page 56), Savory Custards with Wild Nettles (page 24), and/or homemade ice cream or mayo.

makes 12

½ cup (1 stick) unsalted butter

1½ cups almond meal

¾ cup all-purpose flour {GF folks: see page xxi in "Stocking the Pantry" for suggestions}

2 cups confectioners' sugar

½ teaspoon baking powder

½ teaspoon kosher salt

6 egg whites, at room temperature

½ teaspoon almond extract (you can use vanilla extract instead)

Finely grated zest of 1 orange

1 or 2 nectarines, sliced into very thin slivers (feel free to use other seasonal fruit as a topping)

First, make your brown butter by melting the butter over medium-low heat on the stove top. (I suggest using a light-colored saucepan so you can monitor the changing color of your butter.) The butter will bubble, start to smell nice and nutty, and then darken to a golden brown. Remove from the heat and let cool to room temp. You can strain out any funky dark bits and solids, if you choose.

Preheat the oven to 375°F.

Grease a 12-cup muffin pan and set it aside.

Sift the almond meal, flour, sugar, baking powder, and salt into a large bowl. Stir.

In another bowl, use a hand whisk or fork to whisk the egg whites briefly, just until full and frothy.

Fold the egg whites into the dry ingredients. Finally, stir in the brown butter, almond extract, and orange zest.

Scoop the batter into your greased muffin cups. Top each tea cake with a single nectarine sliver. Bake for 20 to 25 minutes, until rich golden brown. (Keep in mind, that a darker muffin tin will cook them more quickly.)

Gently slide a knife around the edge of each friand, then lift it out of the pan to cool on a rack.

raw cashew butter from scratch

I'm in love with cashew butter. I like it both raw and toasted, but I'm particularly enamored with the creamy sweetness of raw cashews. It's hard to find good, raw organic nut butter at the market for less than a fortune, so I decided to make my own.

While I do enjoy my cashew butter raw and unadorned, you can also gussy it up with all sorts of additions. Feel free to toast the nuts before grinding, or add a little honey and/or sea salt to the mix. I find that cashews are so naturally sweet that just a couple of teaspoons of honey are all that's needed.

It's super easy to make nut butters in a food processor. Next time you see those bulk packages of organic nuts, buy a big bag of whatever looks good to you, head home, and make yourself some nut butter. Have fun, experiment, and go for it.

Tip: Sometimes my cashew butter is done after only 4 minute of whirling, but other times the process has taken as long as 12 minutes. Just keep going until you get the consistency you desire.

makes 1 cup

2 cups raw cashews

¼ teaspoon sea salt (optional)

1–2 tablespoons honey (optional)

Sunflower oil, as needed

Place the cashews in a food processor. Add salt and/or honey, if you so desire. Let those blades whirl. At first you'll see the nuts turn to dust. After a few minutes, when the fats are released, they will take on a chunky texture and eventually form a large ball. (You may want to use a spatula to occasionally scrape the sides of your food processor.) If your nut butter seems a little too dry, feel free to add a drizzle of sunflower oil. Keep whirling, and the ball will break down a bit and you'll have smooth, creamy cashew butter—and you made it yourself.

If you plan to eat all of the cashew butter within a few days, you can leave it in a lidded container on your kitchen counter. I warn you, this is a dangerous temptation. Otherwise, store cashew butter in the fridge and let it return to room temp before noshing; the creamy texture will reemerge as it warms.

dehydrated walnuts

I fully credit my mom for teaching me the value of natural foods. She was a foodie hipster before whole foods were even cool.

Recently, when I was visiting Mom in Bolinas, she added some lightly toasted walnuts to our salad and I noticed how particularly good the nuts tasted—the skins lacked the bitterness of most toasted walnuts. Mom told me she had soaked and dehydrated the walnuts.

Not only does dehydrating walnuts make them taste better (by removing much of the tannins), but soaking also purportedly makes the nuts easier to digest by releasing important digestive enzymes and increasing nutritional value. Tasty food that's good for you—thank you, Mom.

Now, I buy big bags of walnuts, soak and re-crisp them in a low oven, and store 'em in the fridge. This dehydrating technique can be used for any nuts, not just walnuts. Once again, I credit Mom with introducing me to a healthy cooking tip.

makes 3 cups

4 cups filtered water

3 cups raw walnuts (11–12 ounces)

2 teaspoons sea salt

Combine the water and sea salt to make a saltwater bath for the walnuts. Soak the nuts for 12 hours or overnight.

Drain the walnuts and transfer them to a baking sheet. If you have a dehydrator, go ahead and use it. If not, place your baking sheet in a low oven (100° to 150°F is ideal) and let the walnuts slowly crisp up. (If you are using an old oven like mine that won't go below 200°F, you will need to prop the door open to achieve a low heat.)

The re-crisping process will take anywhere from 3 to 8 hours, depending on the temperature of your oven. Go ahead and taste the nuts periodically— when the walnuts are firm, dry, and taste delicious, you can pull them from the oven.

Store in an airtight container in the fridge.

fruit

lilah's little apple galettes

Flaky, buttery galettes are a fixture in our gluten-free kitchen. Once you start making them, it's hard to stop. Galettes are flexible for both sweet and savory fillings, plus the rustic beauty of a galette makes for a forgiving recipe, even for beginning bakers. I hope this recipe inspires you to play at home and discover the deliciousness for yourself, gluten-free or not.

My girl, Lilah, loves to help me make galettes. We make dough in advance and keep it in the freezer until we're ready. She layers the apples, shapes the dough, brushes on egg yolk—and sprinkles the sugar, of course!

Because these galettes are low in sugar, I think they make a nice breakfast treat or afternoon pick-me-up. If you do want to serve the galettes for dessert, don't hesitate to add a scoop of vanilla or salted caramel ice cream.

Tip: Be sure to make the dough at least an hour ahead of cooking time, so there's time for it to chill before rolling.

serves 4

Flaky Gluten-Free Pastry Dough
 (page 264)
All-purpose flour, for dusting {GF
 folks: see page xxi in "Stocking
 the Pantry" for suggestions}
4 ripe but firm apples

Juice of 1 lemon
1 egg yolk, whisked
2 tablespoons unsalted butter, melted
2 tablespoons turbinado sugar
¼ teaspoon ground cinnamon

Cut four 12" squares of plastic wrap and lay them on the counter. Use your hands to gently gather the dough into 4 balls. (Don't worry if they aren't exactly the same size; remember that the joy of galettes lies in their imperfect beauty.) Place each ball in the center of a plastic square, then wrap the plastic around the ball and use the heel of your hand to flatten the dough into a thick disk. Chill the dough in the fridge for at least an hour, or up to 2 days. You can also stick wrapped dough in the freezer at this point if you want to save it for later.

When you're ready to bake your galettes, preheat the oven to 375°F. Line a baking sheet with parchment paper.

Take the chilled dough from the fridge. Cover a cutting board with a piece of parchment paper and dust the surface with flour. Place a ball of dough on the parchment and sprinkle a bit of extra flour over the dough. Dust the rolling pin with flour. Roll out the ball of dough into a ⅛"-thick circle. Slide onto the parchment-lined baking sheet. Repeat with remaining dough and return the dough rounds to the fridge while you prep your apples.

Peel and core the apples. Slice them very thinly (use a mandoline, if you've got one) and toss the slices into a bowl with a tablespoon or two of lemon juice.

Take your chilled dough from the fridge and arrange the apple slices in an overlapping, flower-like circular pattern, leaving a 1" to 2" border all around. Fold up this crust border over the arranged fruit and brush with the egg yolk, then drizzle the melted butter onto the uncovered apples. Mix together the sugar and cinnamon and sprinkle over each galette.

Bake the galettes for 35 minutes on the lower rack of the oven, or until the crust is golden brown.

Transfer to a rack until you're ready to serve.

donna's apricot jam with garden rosemary

When Paul first started his jamming obsession six years ago, he walked next door to consult the master. Donna, our neighbor, is an incredible chef, and her jams are always inspired and inspiring. She kindly shared all sorts of jamming tips with Paul and encouraged him to start preserving. She also gave Paul a jar of her amazing apricot-rosemary jam. Herbaceous rosemary is ridiculously good with tangy sweet apricots, and lucky for us all, Donna was willing to share her phenomenal recipe.

Use apricots that are ripe but firm. If your apricots are too juicy, they will make for a mushy jam.

This recipe is not at all labor-intensive, but it is a two-day process.

makes 5 cups

2½ pounds fresh apricots (Blenheim apricots are especially wonderful in this jam)

3¾ cups sugar

Juice of 1 lemon

⅓ cup fresh rosemary leaves, coarsely chopped

Remove the apricot pits and quarter the fruit.

Combine the apricots, sugar, and lemon juice in a stainless steel stockpot or large Dutch oven, stirring regularly as you bring the fruit to a simmer over medium-high heat. (You'll be amazed at how much juice the apricots release as the pot warms.) As soon as the apricots are juicy and bubbling, remove the pan from the heat.

Cut a round of parchment paper and lay it over the apricots while they rest in the pot. Let the fruit cool to room temp, then transfer the covered apricots to the fridge to chill for 12 hours, or overnight.

The next day, place your apricots (in their preserving pot but without the parchment paper) back on the stove top over high heat. Bring the fruit to a boil, stirring gently. Skim off any foam that forms on the top. Boil the apricots over high heat for 5 to 7 minutes, until they have thickened, or reach 221°F on a candy thermometer. Remove the pan from the heat, add the rosemary, and stir gently.

Immediately fill jars with the hot fruit, cover, and let the jam cool to room temp. Store lidded containers in the fridge and eat within 3 weeks. If you'd like to preserve your jam in sealed jars, follow instructions from your favorite jamming guide.

Tip: This jam is delicious on your morning toast, or on the sweet version of Golden Millet Crepes (page 153). And if you try a scoop with a nice slice of cheese, I think you'll fully enjoy the sweet-savory magic of Donna's jam.

backyard figs with prosciutto

Two years ago, we traveled to Italy with our dear friends Abby, Jon, and
Helena. Of course we ate well, but I have to say that the morning I dined on
big ripe figs and paper-thin slices of prosciutto was the highlight. This dish is
not traditionally served for breakfast, but who needs to follow such rules? Eat
figs and prosciutto any time of day, and that's fine by me.

Our fig tree, sprouting right outside our kitchen door, is the happiest
thing in our garden. Less than a decade ago we planted a bare twig of a tree,
and now we have a happy 20-foot-tall beast that threatens to take over the
entire backyard. Cheeky squirrels help themselves to a good portion of the
fruit, but that's okay. I savor every fig we get.

serves 2 to 4

¼ pound prosciutto, thinly sliced
8 plump fresh figs or a dozen little
    guys

Splash of saba or really good aged
    balsamic vinegar (optional)

Serve up a plate of prosciutto and figs. You can even wrap your figs in cloaks
of prosciutto. Drizzle on a little saba or vinegar, if you wish. Take a bite and
enjoy the simple goodness.

pluot parfaits with sweet and crunchy sunflower seeds

The marriage of an apricot and plum makes for delectable offspring. Pluots, with their gorgeous array of colors and juicy texture, are very similar to plums, yet the apricot adds complexity to the flavor. If you can't get Pluots, don't worry; this parfait is also delish with plums, nectarines, peaches, pears, or summer berries.

A parfait is great for breakfast, or as a snack, or really anytime. Make your candied sunflower seeds ahead of time and you can toss together a parfait in minutes. You can also easily pack a parfait for a picnic or kid's lunch.

serves 4

1 cup raw sunflower seeds

½ tablespoon unsalted butter

¼ cup maple sugar (regular cane sugar works fine here as well, but I really like the subtle maple flavor)

Pinch of flaky sea salt

2 cups plain yogurt (I always prefer Greek yogurt)

2 Pluots, pitted and sliced into thin wedges

In a small skillet, cook the sunflower seeds in the butter over medium heat for a minute or two. Add the sugar, and stir briskly until the sugar coats the seeds. Let the seeds continue to cook in the buttery sugar for another 3 to 5 minutes, stirring occasionally, until the seeds are a golden caramel color. Sprinkle on a pinch of sea salt and transfer the seeds to a piece of parchment paper or a plate to cool.

For serving, layer yogurt, candied sunflower seeds, and thinly sliced fruit into low wide glasses or small mason jars. Make sure to get a little of every layer in each bite as you dip your spoon into the parfait: The juicy fruit, creamy yogurt, and crunchy, sweet sunflower seeds work so well together. And if you use maple sugar for the sunflower seeds, it melts into the yogurt in just the right way.

strawberry rhubarb compote with sprigs
of lemon thyme

Strawberries and rhubarb have long been one of my favorite combinations. When I was a young teen, we lived in the California foothills, and Mom would lure me to help harvest in our huge garden by promising to make pies for me. Strawberry rhubarb always sat at the top of my wish list.

This compote is a simple celebration of these compatible friends. Here the fruit is sweet enough to mix with tart unsweetened yogurt while still maintaining the irresistible tang of rhubarb. Swirling compote into creamy Greek yogurt may be all you need for breakfast or a quick snack, or you can add some puffed rice cereal or toasted walnuts to the bowl and you've got a party of flavors and textures at play. The compote is also delicious on Golden Millet Crepes, Sweet or Savory (page 153), Simple Almond Torte with Garden Strawberries + Crème Fraîche (page 199), or swirled into a bowl of simple oatmeal.

. . . .

serves 6 to 8

3½ cups fresh strawberries (1 pound)

12 ounces rhubarb (3 large ribs)

1 cup sugar or ⅔ cup light agave nectar (adjust according to the sweetness of your berries and personal preference)

8 sprigs fresh thyme (optional); lemon thyme is especially good

Preheat the oven to 375°F. Stem the strawberries and quarter any large ones. Smaller berries can be halved or left whole. Place in a medium ovenproof baking dish (11" x 7" or 9"x 9").

Trim ragged ends from your rhubarb. Slice the ribs horizontally into ¼"-thick crescents. Add the rhubarb to the baking dish. Pour the sugar or agave nectar over the fruit and toss to coat. Nestle in the thyme sprigs, if you like.

Bake in the center of the oven for 35 to 40 minutes, until the strawberries and rhubarb are tender and juicy. Let the compote cool, then remove the thyme branches, letting the tiny leaves fall into the roasted fruit at will.

Store the compote in the fridge in a lidded container for up to a week.

french toast sandwiches with peaches and fresh mozzarella

Sandwiched between two slices of French toast, peaches get juicy and sweet in the hot oven, and are oh so good with warm, melty mozzarella. Add a drizzle of maple syrup . . . yum!

While I am partial to the peach and mozz combination, you can make these sandwiches with all sorts of other fillings—baking French toast is an easy way to feed a crowd for breakfast or brunch. In the winter, try sliced pears with mozzarella or even Parmesan. You can also stuff French toast sandwiches with jam and cream cheese any time of year.

makes 4

2 eggs

½ cup milk

1 tablespoon maple syrup, plus more, warm, for serving

½ teaspoon vanilla extract

Pinch of sea salt

Sprinkle of ground cinnamon

8 slices sandwich bread {GF folks: see page xxii in "Stocking the Pantry" for suggestions}

4 tablespoons salted butter

3–4 ounces fresh buffalo or cow's milk mozzarella, thinly sliced

1 peach, pitted and sliced into 16 thin wedges

Preheat the oven to 375°F. Generously coat a large baking sheet with butter.

In a wide shallow bowl, whisk together the eggs, milk, maple syrup, vanilla, salt, and cinnamon.

Submerge each slice of bread in the eggy batter for 30 seconds or so. You want to coat the bread but not let it get soggy. Place all 8 slices of battered bread onto your greased baking sheet. Bake in the hot oven for 10 minutes.

Remove the baking sheet from the oven and flip all the slices of bread. Tuck a nub (teaspoon or so) of butter under each slice of toast before returning the baking sheet to the oven. Top half of the bread slices with a layer of mozzarella and four peach wedges. Continue to bake for 8 to 10 minutes, until all the toast is golden brown and the mozzarella is nice and melty.

Assemble the sandwiches and generously drizzle warm maple syrup over the top. Serve right away.

nectarine blackberry crumble with hazelnut crunch

This recipe is all about the bounty of summer fruit. I am particularly fond of combining nectarines and blackberries, but I hope you'll have fun and use the crumble topping on whatever goodies you have in abundance; pluots, peaches, pears, and all sorts of berries can be used as a base. Simply adjust the amount of agave you toss with the filling, depending on the natural sweetness of the fruit you choose. For example, if you are using only blackberries, which have a low natural sugar content, you may want to double or even triple the amount of agave.

You won't find any refined white sugar here, and hazelnuts add a good dose of protein, so I don't feel guilty serving this crumble for breakfast. No one else in our house seems to be complaining either.

....

serves 8 to 10

crumble topping:

¾ cup raw hazelnuts

¾ cup all-purpose flour {GF folks: see page xxi in "Stocking the Pantry" for suggestions}

½ cup coconut sugar (you can substitute light brown sugar here)

Pinch of sea salt

6 tablespoons cold unsalted butter

fruit filling:

6 nectarines, sliced

2 cups fresh blackberries

2 tablespoons light agave nectar

1 tablespoon freshly squeezed lemon juice

1 teaspoon vanilla extract

1 tablespoon all-purpose flour {GF folks: see page xxi in "Stocking the Pantry" for suggestions}

for serving:

Chilled heavy cream

Preheat the oven to 375°F.

For the topping: Lightly toast the hazelnuts on a baking sheet in the oven for 6 to 8 minutes. Let cool, then rub off skins. Place the hazelnuts in a waxed paper or regular paper bag and use a rolling pin or meat tenderizer to crush

them; you want a coarse, crumbly texture with some nice big chunks of hazelnut. A large mortar and pestle will also do the trick.

In a large bowl, stir together the flour, coconut sugar, and salt. Cut the chilled butter into small chunks and add it to the dry ingredients. Mix everything together with your hands until the butter has broken down to smallish bits. Add the crushed hazelnuts to the bowl, and continue using your hands to mix everything until you have a coarse crumble. Place the topping in the freezer to chill while you prep your fruit.

For the filling: In a 13" x 9" baking dish, gently toss the nectarines and berries with the agave nectar, lemon juice, vanilla, and flour. Scatter the chilled topping over the fruit.

Bake for 35 to 40 minutes, until the berries are juicy and bubbling and the topping is golden brown. Let the crumble cool for 15 minutes before serving so the juices have a chance to thicken a bit.

Serve the crumble warm or at room temperature, scooped into shallow bowls. Pass a pitcher of cold heavy cream around the table to liberally pour over the crumble.

pears poached in lillet

Oh, I love Lillet, a delectably fruity fortified wine from France. Every time I sip a Lillet on the rocks with a twist, I feel celebratory. This recipe takes my love for this simple aperitif and infuses the deliciousness into pears as they poach. The light, perfumy, pear flavor is heightened by the Lillet, while additions of thyme, citrus, and peppercorns give an earthy grounding to this light dessert.

The pears are absolutely beautiful served in individual bowls to dinner guests.

....

serves 4 (if you want a smaller dessert—enough to serve 8—cut the pears in half just before serving)

3 cups white Lillet

2 cups water

Zest and juice of 1 orange

¾ cup sugar or ½ cup light agave
    nectar

2 small tangerines or 8 kumquats,
    thinly sliced, with the peels still on

10 sprigs fresh thyme

8 black peppercorns

4 just-ripe pears (Warren, Anjou,
    or Bosc)

Place the Lillet, water, orange zest, orange juice, sugar, tangerines, thyme, and peppercorns into a large saucepan. Heat over medium-high heat for a few minutes, stirring occasionally, until the sugar dissolves.

In the meantime, peel the pears and cut a bit off the bottom of each to make it flat and able to stand without falling. (Come serving time, you will appreciate a pear that can stand up.) Keep the stems intact.

Submerge your peeled pears in the poaching liquid and return to a simmer. Cut out a circle of parchment paper to cover the pears and liquid. Place a plate or small pot lid over the parchment-covered pears to keep them submerged. If your pears are not totally covered by liquid, you may want to add a bit more water or just rotate the fruit periodically to ensure even cooking.

Simmer the covered pears for 30 minutes. (If your pears are a little underripe, you may want to add 10 or so minutes to the cooking time. If the

pears are very ripe, 20 minutes of poaching should be enough.) To test for doneness, a sharp knife should be able to pierce a pear without effort. Remove the pan from the stove top and let the pears sit, covered and submerged in their poaching liquid, for 20 to 30 minutes before serving.

Place each pear in a small pretty bowl or glass. Strain the poaching liquid and keep all the goodies, setting them aside for garnish. Pour some strained liquid over each pear. Add a couple of poached citrus slices, a twig of two of thyme, and some orange zest to each bowl.

raspberry fool

The British have been whipping up fools for 500 years. Talk about old school! Fruit and whipped cream are a classic combo, and now you can feel anchored in tradition as you swirl the two yummy ingredients together in pretty glasses and serve up fools for dessert. I like to think the fool has survived because it would be foolish to let such a simple delight become obsolete.

Try to use the best-quality cream and the ripest berries you can find. With such a simple concoction, the caliber of ingredients really makes the dish.

serves 4

1 cup fresh raspberries (blackberries and/or strawberries are good alternatives)

2 tablespoons light agave nectar (granulated sugar works as well)

1 cup chilled heavy cream

1–2 tablespoons confectioners' sugar

1½ teaspoons Grand Marnier

In a small bowl, mix the raspberries and agave nectar. Smash the berries with the back of a fork to make a loose, sweet puree. Let the berries macerate for 30 minutes. Meanwhile, chill a bowl for the whipped cream.

In the chilled bowl, whip the heavy cream until soft peaks form. Mix in the confectioners' sugar and Grand Marnier. Finish whipping the sweet and slightly boozy cream; I suggest keeping the whipped cream soft and billowy, just firm enough to hold its shape.

Gently fold the berry puree into the cream. (If you swirl in a spoonful of puree at a time, you get a nice marbled effect.)

Scoop the fool into pretty glasses. You can eat right away, or cover and refrigerate the fools for a few hours, until dessert time.

Tip: You may want to serve your fools with a side of crunchy cookies. Pistachio Tangerine Sugar Cookies (page 201) would be delicious.

honeydew granita with lemon verbena and lime

I often think of the role color plays in our food choices and desires. A flash of red warns of fiery spice within a chile pepper, while leafy greens call to our instincts when we crave freshness. I know I'm deeply swayed by color when it comes to cooking, and every trip to the market is a visual feast enticing the omnivore in me. From the deep greens of rainbow chard leaves contrasting with their jewel-toned stems to sunny lemons, to dark crimson cherries, and the pinkest king salmon, it all inspires me to get cooking—and eating.

I'm not sure which came first, my love of honeydew melon or pale milky green as my favorite color. For me, honeydew green connotes a soft, fresh sweetness, and those are the words I'd use to describe the taste of this granita. The honest melon flavor is the star of the show, while the herbs and citrus are kind supporting actors in both flavor and color.

serves 6 to 8

1 cup water

12 fresh lemon verbena leaves (fresh mint leaves are an easier-to-find substitute)

1 medium honeydew melon

½ cup freshly squeezed lime juice

¾ cup light agave nectar or 1 cup superfine sugar (if your melon is super sweet, cut back on sweetener)

Bring the water to a boil and pour it over the lemon verbena or mint leaves in a bowl. Cover and let steep for 20 to 30 minutes, then discard the leaves.

Cut the melon open and scrape out the seeds, but don't discard the tender, pale flesh surrounding the seeds—it's so sweet and tasty. Remove the rinds and cut the melon into chunks. You want about 4 cups chopped melon.

Using a standing blender or food processor, blend the verbena infusion, melon chunks, lime juice, and agave or sugar. (I like to do a couple of batches in my blender.) Pour the puree into a large bowl and give it a stir. Taste the pale green deliciousness and feel free to add a little more agave or sugar if your melon isn't super sweet, keeping in mind that sweetness diminishes with freezing. Your puree can be made up to 24 hours before you want to freeze it. I usually let it chill in the fridge overnight.

Pour the puree into a shallow baking dish. Cover and freeze for
45 minutes to 1 hour. Remove the dish from the freezer and stir with a fork to
break up any frozen bits. Make sure to scrape the edges of the pan—this is
where freezing begins. Continue to freeze in 45-minute intervals, interspersed
with scraping and freezing again. After a few hours of freezing and scraping,
your granita should be ready to eat. (If you forget to stir and the granita
solidifies, don't worry; you can use a fork to scrape frozen granita and the
texture will still be fantastic!)

The granita keeps in the freezer for 2 weeks.

pears with stilton + honeycomb

This plate feels just right in the early fall, when juicy pears have just come into season and still maintain the lure of an exotic treat. A slab of salty, pungent Stilton makes a good partner to the silky sweetness of the fruit. And nature doesn't get much more festive than gorgeous honeycomb.

When we have people over for supper, it's always nice to have a little indulgence after the meal . . . maybe some good coffee, a tisane, a glass of port, and something sweet, of course. Sometimes caramel sundaes are in order, other nights it's a fruit galette. I have a few friends who don't like sugary desserts, and this pear platter satisfies those with a sweet tooth, while still attending to those folks who aren't sugar fiends.

{A GF Note on Stilton: There is debate as to whether Stilton and some other blue cheeses are truly gluten-free, as they are often made with cultures from bread mold, though the cheese does pass measurable gluten-free standards. In my personal experience, I can tolerate Stilton without issue, but if you want to be absolutely careful, you may want to opt for another cheese.}

Tip: Well, if you haven't tried honeycomb, go out and find some. Maybe you need to invite some friends over for an excuse—it's more fun that way, right? Honeycomb is available at most specialty food stores. Or if you happen to have a beekeeping neighbor, ask if he or she will part with a square for you. I first tried honeycomb in New Zealand years ago and fell in love. First of all, its natural geometric charm cannot be denied. Second, the beauty is packed with fresh honey and is a fun waxy treat to chew on. After you savor the honey, you are left chewing the waxy remains; chew for a while if you are a gum lover like me, or discard the wax and keep eating the other goodies.

serves 6

6 juicy pears

1 (5-ounce) piece honeycomb

1 (8-ounce) wedge Stilton {folks with severe gluten intolerance or celiac disease, check with the cheese producer to ensure the cheese is safe to eat}

Small bowl of Toasty Pecans with Garden Rosemary, Honey, and Smoked Salt (optional; page 190)

Get out a big, beautiful platter or cutting board, and have some fun arranging your pears, honeycomb, and Stilton, while keeping it loose and simple. Cut up all the elements or leave them whole—up to you. Let the ingredients speak for themselves. Add the pecans to the arrangement, if you like.

This is the kind of plate that can accommodate some crackers on the side, but you really don't need them when you have three such special ingredients to enjoy. Just pass some small plates around the table and let everyone serve themselves.

boozy cherries with port, honey, and bay

When cherries come to market, we buy up as many as we can. Mostly we eat the cherries in their natural state and devour them with abandon, sometimes until our bellies beg us to stop. If you want to prolong the joy of cherries just a bit and are interested in a sultry and decadent, yet simple, treat, this recipe is for you. Scoop a few of these boozy cherries over vanilla ice cream, splash on some of the herby cherry-infused port, and you won't be sorry.

A jar of these cherries makes a great hostess gift.

Tip: I'm not big into kitchen gadgets, but a cherry/olive pitter makes me so happy with the time and effort it saves.

makes about 2 cups

1½ cups fresh dark red cherries

1 cup port

¼ cup honey

1 teaspoon vanilla extract

1 dried bay leaf

First, remove the cherry pits.

Heat the port, honey, vanilla, and bay leaf in a small deep saucepan over medium-high heat until simmering. Add the cherries to the warm liquid, and adjust the heat to achieve a gentle simmer for 3 minutes to warm the cherries through and help them to soak up the boozy goodness.

Remove the pan from the heat and scoop the cherries into a mason jar. Pour the hot, infused port over the cherries and let all flavors mingle as they cool to room temp.

Cover the mason jar, refrigerate, and enjoy within 3 weeks.

Tip: Serve the cherries on top of vanilla ice cream, or if you can't eat dairy, try a scoop of Coconut Bliss. These cherries are also amazing on top of my Simple Almond Torte (page 199); use them instead of the strawberries, but do include a nice dollop of crème fraîche.

preserved lemons

Preserved lemons add great tang and acid to all sorts of things from baked chicken to salad dressing to pastas. They are a wonderful homemade condiment to have on hand. Years ago, my neighbor Rich brought over a jar of his own preserved Meyer lemons. I'd always been a fan of the concentrated, salty citrus flavor of preserved lemons in Moroccan dishes, and as a lover of anything lemony, I thoroughly enjoyed playing with this ingredient new to my kitchen. Rich loaned me his copy Ghillie Basan's beautiful book *Modern Moroccan*, which got me started making my own preserved lemons. I've been making them ever since.

Try out your preserved lemons in my French Lentils with Preserved Lemon, Tarragon, and Creamy Goat Cheese (page 72). Remember, when you cook with preserved lemons, be sure to use only the peels and to give them a good rinse to remove the excess salty brine.

makes 2 to 3 pints

10 Meyer or Eureka lemons (use organic, please)

¾ cup kosher salt

Thoroughly rinse the lemons under cool running water and give the skins a good scrub.

Get out 2 or 3 clean pint-size jars. (How many jars you need will depend on the size of your lemons.)

Use a sharp knife to cut the lemons: You want to approach each lemon as if you were going to quarter it lengthwise, but stop cutting about three-quarters of the way through so that ½" of the lemon remains intact.

Stuff the cavity of each lemon with plenty of salt, at least 1 tablespoon per lemon. Tightly pack the lemons into the jars, leaving a bit of headspace at the top of each jar. Use the back of a spoon to squash the lemons nice and tight. (If the lemons at the top of the jar are not covered in liquid after the squashing, use a little additional lemon juice to provide cover.)

Cover the jars and leave them on the counter at room temperature for a couple of days. Then use a spoon to again push the lemons down into their preserving liquid. Store the jars in the fridge, and your lemons will be cured and ready for use after 1 month.

Preserved lemons will keep for many months in the fridge.

blood orange granita with tangerine and cardamom

When blood oranges make their annual debut just after New Year, I cannot resist. In the midst of deep winter, when gray days seem to end way too quickly, the vibrant sunset hues of blood oranges always bring me cheer, delight, and hope for the year ahead.

There is magic in that deep red flesh, and this granita recipe fully celebrates the fruit's ruby color. Mixed with sweet tangerines, cardamom, and a splash of rum, blood oranges are transformed into a refreshing and light dessert.

Making granita is ridiculously simple, and if you have a few hours on a weekend afternoon to occasionally stir the slowly freezing concoction, you will be greatly rewarded. Keep in mind: The shallower the pan (and bigger the surface area), the quicker the freeze. Using a sheet pan will make for the fastest freeze.

....

serves 3 or 4

4 or 5 blood oranges

4–6 sweet and juicy tangerines

¾ cup sugar or ½ cup light agave nectar

5 cardamom pods, slightly crushed to release the flavor

1 tablespoon rum

Squeeze the citrus until you have 2 cups juice.

Place the citrus juice, sugar or agave, cardamom pods, and rum in a medium heavy-bottom saucepan. Over medium-high heat, cook to dissolve the sugar, stirring constantly. When the sugar has dissolved, remove the pan from the heat. Let the liquid sit for 15 minutes, then strain out the cardamom pods and seeds. Cool the liquid completely in the fridge, even overnight. (This mixture can be made up to 48 hours before you want to freeze it. I usually chill it overnight.)

Pour the liquid into a shallow baking pan. Freeze for 45 minutes to 1 hour. Remove the pan from the freezer and use a fork to stir and break up any frozen bits. Make sure to scrape the edges of the pan—this is where the freezing begins.

Continue to freeze in 45-minute intervals, stirring and scraping and freezing again. After a few hours of freezing and stirring, your granita should

fruit

be ready to eat. (If you forget to stir regularly and the granita solidifies, don't worry; you can always use a fork to scrape the icy block and the texture will still be wonderful.)

Once you are ready to eat the granita, scoop it into small glasses or bowls, and serve immediately. It melts quickly. You can add a dollop of whipped cream or a cookie on the side if you choose. The additions are decadently delicious, yet in truth this granita easily holds its own as the bright end to a meal.

The granita keeps in the freezer for 2 weeks.

kid
favorites

froyo pops with blueberries and greek yogurt

I started making froyo popsicles as a way to get calcium and good yogurt cultures into my little girl, who wanted nothing to do with drinking milk or eating yogurt. Unable to resist homemade pops packed with yogurt and fruit, she gobbled them down. So did I.

Feel free to use honey, sugar, or the sweetener of your choice here. I prefer the easy sweetness of light agave nectar in this recipe. Keep in mind that these pops are not super sweet—I really like when the tang of yogurt still comes through loud and clear. If you prefer your pops a little sweeter, go ahead and sweeten the yogurt to your liking.

Tip: If you don't tolerate cow's milk, give sheep's milk yogurt a try. It makes for delicious popsicles.

makes 10

1 cup fresh or frozen blueberries

1 teaspoon finely grated lemon zest

1–1¼ cups light agave nectar

2¼ cups plain Greek yogurt

In a small saucepan, mix together the blueberries, lemon zest, and ½ cup of the agave nectar. Simmer gently for 10 minutes, or until the blueberries have softened into the sweet syrup. Chill the blueberry sauce in the fridge until fully cooled.

Once the blueberries have cooled, get out a medium bowl and whisk together the yogurt and the remaining ½ to ¾ cup agave, depending on your sweet tooth. Lightly swirl the blueberry syrup into the yogurt so the popsicles have a nice marbled look. Scoop the fruit and yogurt into 10 3-ounce ice-pop molds and freeze until solid.

Feel free to serve up froyo pops for breakfast. Why not?

otis's ice cream pie with cookie dough crust

Please forgive me—there is no restraint to be found in this hedonistic creation. My son, Otis, introduced our family to the concept of ice cream pie, and for years now, we've been experimenting with such recipes by crumbling store-bought cookies and mashing them with butter to make a crust, then scooping our favorite ice cream on top. Of course that's all good, but Otis has boldly taken ice cream pie to a new height of indulgence. If you are a fan of cookie dough ice cream, you will freak for this pie.

I asked Otis what kind of cookies he wanted for the ice cream pie we were planning to make for his 12th birthday, and he said, "What about a cookie dough crust?" "Hell yeah!" I replied, proud of my kid and his decadent instincts.

Now all the kids we know beg us to make Otis's Ice Cream Pie for their birthdays. This pie is kid heaven.

....

serves 8

½ cup loosely packed light brown sugar

¼ cup granulated sugar

½ cup (1 stick) unsalted butter, softened

1 egg*

1 teaspoon vanilla extract

1 cup all-purpose flour {GF folks: see page xxi "Stocking the Pantry" for suggestions}

Pinch of salt

1¼ cups chocolate chips

1 quart vanilla ice cream

Whipped cream and chocolate shavings, for topping (optional)

In a standing mixer with the paddle attachment, or a large bowl with a hand mixer, cream together both sugars and the butter. Next, add the egg and vanilla and mix. With the mixer running, slowly add the flour and salt to the bowl until everything is well blended. Finally, mix in the chocolate chips.

Using the back of a spoon and/or your fingertips, press the cookie dough into the bottom and around the sides of a standard pie pan to make a crust for your pie. Cover and chill in the freezer for 45 minutes.

Take into account that there's raw egg in this recipe, and make the pie at your own discretion.

Once the crust is firm, take the ice cream out of the freezer to soften it a bit. When the ice cream is spreadable, take your pie pan from the freezer and spread a nice thick layer of ice cream onto the cookie dough crust. Cover again, and return the pie to the freezer until both dough and ice cream are chilled and firmed up, at least another 30 minutes. Top with whipped cream and chocolate shavings if you so desire . . . and maybe a few birthday candles.

Eat any leftovers within 3 days.

brown sugar caramel corn

Caramel corn is dangerous for me. Dangerous in that one nibble of the crunchy sweet saltiness leads to the next, and before I know it, the entire batch has disappeared. It's no surprise that Paul and the kids feel the same way and are always game to make a batch of caramel corn with me.

makes 10 cups

½ cup popcorn kernels

½ cup loosely packed light brown sugar

2 tablespoons water

4 tablespoons cold unsalted butter, cut into ½" chunks

2 tablespoons heavy cream

1 teaspoon vanilla extract

Generous pinch of Maldon sea salt or fleur de sel

1 cup whole salted roasted peanuts or coarsely chopped roasted salted Marcona almonds (optional)

Preheat the oven to 250°F. Line a large baking sheet with parchment paper.

Pop your popcorn, and transfer it to an extra-large bowl (you'll have about 10 cups).

Next, make the caramel sauce. (Have your prepped ingredients next to the stove top, ready to use.) Place the brown sugar in a small, heavy-bottom saucepan. Pour the water evenly over the sugar. Turn the stove top to medium-high heat. Hold the saucepan by the handle and swirl it occasionally until the sugar has dissolved. (It's essential to avoid letting the sugar burn until it has completely dissolved.) Cover the pan and turn the heat to high. Boil for 2 minutes, then remove the lid and swirl the pan occasionally until the caramel thickens, begins to smoke, and you can smell the emerging caramel. (Be sure to let your caramel get to this smoking phase—caramel isn't caramel until the sugar burns.) Let the caramel smoke for 15 seconds, then remove the pan from the heat.

Immediately, whisk the butter and cream into the caramel. Stir in the vanilla and salt, and your caramel is done.

Pour the hot caramel over the popped corn. Add the nuts if you like, and toss until everything is coated in caramel. (Be careful not to burn yourself on the hot caramel—use tongs or spoons to mix ingredients.) Taste for seasoning, and add a little more salt if you think it needs it.

Spread the sticky corn and nuts onto the baking sheet. Bake for 30 minutes. Let the caramel corn cool for a few minutes, until it firms up. Dig in.

If you happen to have any leftovers, I'm guessing the caramel corn could be stored in an airtight container for a day or two. That's the kind of restraint we have never found.

crème fraîche caramel sauce

Ah, burnt sugar, we love you so!

I've found that caramel sundaes never fail as an easy dessert to please a crowd. Once you've made your own caramel sauce, you can whip up decadent sundaes with total abandon. If you like Marcona almonds on your sundaes, as I do, go for it—their salty crunch makes for an amazingly tasty companion to the smooth, dark caramel. You can also drizzle caramel over sliced pears or onto a fruit galette (see page 210).

This caramel has an exceptional richness thanks to the turbinado sugar, while crème fraîche lends a subtle and unusual tang.

makes about 2 cups

1½ cups turbinado sugar

⅓ cup water

10 tablespoons cold unsalted butter, cut into ½" chunks

⅔ cup crème fraîche (see page 266 for making your own)

1 tablespoon vanilla bean paste or vanilla extract

½–1 teaspoon Maldon or any other nice sea salt

Set all prepped ingredients next to your stove top.

First, place the sugar in a medium, deep, heavy-bottom saucepan and drizzle on the water, just to wet the sugar. Turn the heat to medium (or medium-low if your stove runs hot), and give the handle an occasional shake to stir the sugar as it melts. Please don't let the sugar caramelize until it has fully dissolved. Once the sugar crystals have melted completely, turn up the heat to high and let the liquid bubble vigorously. (When making caramel, please be careful of splattering. Hot caramel really burns.)

After about 4 minutes of boiling, the sugar will smoke a bit, you will smell the emerging caramel, and the sauce at the edges of pan will turn dark brown. Let the caramel continue to smoke for 15 to 30 seconds, then pull the pan off the stove top. Immediately whisk in the cold butter. Next, add the crème fraîche and keep whisking. Finally, add the vanilla and salt, and you're good to go.

Whatever caramel you don't eat right away, transfer to a lidded container and keep in the fridge for up to a month. Rewarm the sauce just before serving.

peanut butter cups with dark chocolate + flaky sea salt

Top-notch chocolate, good organic peanut butter, and flaky sea salt elevate this already beloved treat to a new height of irresistibility.

I like making these PB cups in very small papers; with the richness of the ingredients, a bite-size nibble feels just right. With the tiny cups, it's a little tricky getting the chocolate to fully coat the sides, so don't worry if a bit of peanut butter peeks through.

makes 24

½ cup salted, unsweetened crunchy peanut butter

3 tablespoons confectioners' sugar

2 cups chopped semisweet chocolate or 60% dark chocolate

Flaky sea salt

In a small bowl, use a fork to thoroughly mix the peanut butter and sugar. Refrigerate.

Fashion a double boiler for melting the chocolate. I nestle a metal bowl above a pot of hot, but not boiling, water. (Be careful to slowly melt your chocolate—too much heat can burn and ruin it. And don't allow even the tiniest splash of water to touch the chocolate, or it will seize up and never melt.)

Place 48 mini (1") baking cups onto a tray or baking sheet, doubling them up so you have 24 cups. Doubling the papers makes for extra stability.

Pour a little less than ½ teaspoon of the melted chocolate into each mini baking cup—just enough to coat the bottoms with a thin layer of chocolate. Let cool in the refrigerator for 15 minutes.

Scoop 24 teaspoon-size balls of peanut butter into the centers of each baking cup, on top of the chilled chocolate base. Keep in mind that the peanut butter mound should be narrow enough to allow another layer of chocolate to ooze down around the edges.

Pour melted chocolate over the tops and down around the sides of the peanut butter to enclose it. Sprinkle a few flakes of sea salt over each peanut butter cup. Refrigerate again until firm.

That is one tasty bite!

The peanut butter cups can be stored at room temp in an airtight container. Eat within a few days.

quick and easy peppermint bark

We try to keep the holidays low-key at our house. The kids love opening their Advent calendars, hanging stripy hand-knit stocking from the mantle, picking out just the right Christmas tree and loading it up with the funky array of ornaments we've accumulated over the years. One tradition Otis and Lilah look forward to every year is making peppermint bark. Creating their own holiday candy feels like magic to them. Who can deny chocolate-peppermint magic to a kid? Not me.

Pack peppermint bark into little tins or mason jars, and you've got instant presents to give to teachers, colleagues, family, and friends.

makes 1¾ pounds

1 pound semisweet or bittersweet
   chocolate

12 ounces white chocolate

3 or 4 medium peppermint
   candy canes

Use a sharp knife to chop the semisweet or bittersweet chocolate into little slivers. In a double boiler, melt the chocolate until smooth and silky. (A couple of things to remember when melting chocolate: Be extra careful to gently melt the chocolate, because it will be ruined if it burns. And don't let even a drop of water mix with the chocolate or it will seize into a ball and refuse to melt.) While the chocolate is melting, line a large baking sheet with parchment paper.

Pour the melted chocolate onto your parchment-lined baking sheet. Use the back of a spoon or spatula to spread the chocolate around until it makes a ⅛"-thick layer. Stick the baking sheet in the fridge for 15 to 20 minutes, allowing the chocolate to firm up.

While the base layer of chocolate is cooling, chop and melt the white chocolate in the same gentle fashion as you did the darker chocolate. (Again, go slowly and remember not to get a splash of water in the chocolate.)

Go ahead and crush your candy canes. (With my kids itching to help: I stick the candy into a sturdy resealable plastic bag and let the kiddos toss it onto the floor and watch the candy shatter.)

Once the darker chocolate has firmed up a bit in the fridge and the white chocolate has melted, pour the white chocolate over the dark. Again, use the back of a spoon to create a relatively smooth layer. If the base chocolate layer melts a bit into the white, swirl this hint of darker chocolate for a slightly marbled look. Sprinkle the crushed candy canes onto the warm white chocolate. Return the baking sheet to the fridge and let your peppermint bark chill for a couple of hours or even overnight.

Once fully chilled and firm, peppermint bark can be broken into pieces using your hands or a heavy knife. Store in an airtight container and eat within 2 weeks.

odds + ends

the simple pleasure of a pot of beans

I could write an entire book about the uses for a good flavorful pot of beans, the ultimate in inexpensive nourishment. There is an amazing range of dried beans available, and each heirloom variety has its own distinct flavor, texture, and beauty. We tend to make a pot of beans a week, and the satisfaction lasts and lasts. For a quick weeknight supper, we'll eat warm bowls of beans mixed with sautéed greens, chopped avocado, and salsa. Sometimes, I'll add half the cooked beans to a hearty stew (like my Cozy Winter Soup with Fennel Sausage, Leeks, White Beans, and Rapini on page 119) and then freeze the rest for later use. You can also refry the beans with bacon or chorizo, or simply top them with a generous handful of snipped fresh herbs. Roll a scoop of velvety beans in a warm corn tortilla, and everyone is happy.

I hope I can encourage you to make your own beans and that this simple recipe will become your own. I can't think of a more satisfying way to feed a hungry belly.

....

1 pound dried beans (cannellini and Midnight black beans are always favorites around here, but there are so many other tempting heirloom varieties that I like to switch it up)

1 head garlic, cloves separated and peeled

1 dried bay leaf or ½ teaspoon ground epazote

1 tablespoon smoked sea salt (regular sea salt will do, but the smoked salt turns a pot of beans into something really special)

Thoroughly rinse the beans under cool tap water, then place in a stockpot or Dutch oven. Cover with ample cool water, at least 3" to 4" above the beans. Let the beans soak at room temperature overnight.

When you're ready to cook the next day, make sure that your beans are covered by at least 2" of water. There's no need to drain the soaking water if it still looks clear; just pour in a little more. Bring the liquid to a boil, then turn the heat down to maintain a nice simmer. Skim off any foam that forms on the surface. After you are done skimming the foam, add the garlic, bay leaf or epazote, and smoked salt to the pot. Partially cover the pot, and let those beans simmer away gently.

While the beans cook, make sure at least 1" of water is covering the little guys during the entire cooking process. Add more liquid as needed. Don't worry about having extra water when your beans are done cooking, because that liquid can be used in a good bean soup.

Cook the beans until tender. Cooking time will vary depending on the type, size, and age of the bean, and can be anywhere from 45 minutes to 2½ hours. Fish out and discard the bay leaf before serving.

bread crumbs and croutons

A while back, I shared a recipe on my blog that called for bread crumbs. I assumed that any gluten-free cook would know to use gluten-free bread crumbs. I was wrong. Many people seemed baffled by the idea of gluten-free bread crumbs, not knowing where to get such a thing or even imagining gluten-free bread crumbs existed. I realized I had some explaining to do.

I have always made my own bread crumbs and croutons—long before I had to go gluten-free. The technique is exactly the same, and the only difference is that I now use gluten-free bread. Not only are homemade bread crumbs and croutons easy to make, but they also taste infinitely better than any prepackaged variety.

For croutons, I buy bread specifically for the task, but for bread crumbs I use leftover butt ends from our standard sandwich bread. I always keep a bag of end pieces in my freezer so I can make bread crumbs to order without having to take a trip to the market. Scraps that go to delicious use make me happy.

bread crumbs:

Preheat the oven to 300°F. Place few slices of {gluten-free} bread, or those lonely end pieces, in the oven for about 15 minutes, until the bread is dry. Tear the dry bread into chunks and toss them into a standing blender until you've loosely filled it with no more than 2 cups. Pulse a few times and you've got basic homemade bread crumbs. Continue making batches of bread crumbs without over-packing the blender. Feel free to add chopped herbs to the mix, or you can toast up your bread crumbs with a little butter in a skillet, if you're feeling decadent.

3 cups loosely packed torn pieces
  {gluten-free} bread (a crusty rustic
  loaf or baguette-style bread is best,
  though in a pinch, I use doughy
  hamburger buns . . . don't tell)

2 tablespoons olive oil

Pinch of sea salt

1 clove garlic, halved (optional)

Preheat the oven to 375°F. Distribute the torn bread chunks onto a baking sheet, drizzle with the olive oil, and sprinkle with sea salt. (Feel free to make small or large croutons depending on your preference.) Toss to coat.

Bake for 8 to 14 minutes, until golden and crispy on the outside. Cooking time will vary depending on the size of your croutons.

If you want your croutons garlicky, rub the hot croutons with the halved garlic just after they come out of the oven.

flaky gluten-free pastry dough

This is the basic dough recipe I use for all my galettes and tarts, both sweet and savory. I like the toothsome quality of Pamela's brilliant gluten-free flour blend. (Keep in mind that there is a slight sweetness to the flour blend.)

makes enough for 1 big galette/tart or 4 little galettes/tarts

1½ cups Pamela's Gluten-Free Bread
   Mix

Pinch of sea salt

6 tablespoons cold unsalted butter

5–7 tablespoons ice water

Place the flour and salt in a large bowl and stir. Cut the butter into small pieces and add them to the bowl. Using a pastry cutter or 2 forks, cut the butter into the flour mix. Keep going until the butter is reduced to pea-size bits. Drizzle 5 tablespoons of the ice water into the bowl and continue to mix the ingredients with the pastry cutter. Even though the mixture will still be quite crumbly at this point, squeeze some dough between your fingers and see if it holds together. You will probably need to add another tablespoon or two of ice water to get your dough to hold together. Note: Don't overwork or over-wet your dough: A slightly crumbly dough, with smears of butter throughout, will give you a great flaky crust later.

For a single large tart or galette, cut a large square of plastic wrap and lay it on the countertop. Use your hands to gently gather the dough into a ball and place it in the center of the plastic; wrap it up and use the heel of your hand to flatten the dough into a thick round.

For 4 smaller tarts or galettes, use 4 smaller pieces of plastic and wrap the rounds of dough individually.

Chill the wrapped dough in the fridge for at least 1 hour, or up to 2 days. You can also stick the wrapped dough in the freezer at this point if you want to save it for later.

A few words of wisdom about rolling out dough: If you are anything like me, by which I mean not a natural baker who can roll dough in her sleep, be patient with yourself. I have found myself cursing with frustration as I roll out dough. A few tricks have helped to ease my pain. First, you can always roll dough between 2 pieces of parchment paper. Second, if your dough seems to be getting a bit sticky and unmanageable, stick it back into the fridge to firm up for a few minutes. Third, if rolling dough is just too much to ask, you can press dough into a buttered tart pan, then return the pan to the fridge to re-chill the dough before assembling your tart.

Even with my own frustrations rolling out dough, the resulting tart or galette makes any aggravation so worthwhile.

homemade crème fraîche

A decade ago, my mother-in-law encouraged me to start making my own crème fraîche, and she was right. There's no reason not to take on such a simple task. Go for it—you won't regret it. Once we have a luscious jar of crème fraîche in the fridge, I find myself slathering it onto waffles with peaches, onto crepes with berries, and into veggie soups. Dangerously good stuff!

makes 1¼ cups

1 cup heavy cream (not ultra-pasteurized)

2 tablespoons cultured buttermilk

Pour the cream and buttermilk into a clean jar. Mix well. Loosely cover the jar with cheesecloth or a clean kitchen towel, and let the mixture sit on your counter at room temperature for 24 to 48 hours. Watch it thicken. . . .

After a day or two, when the cream has thickened to your liking, cover the jar tightly and refrigerate. Keep in mind that the cream will continue to thicken up a bit more once it has chilled. Crème fraîche will keep for a couple of weeks if stored in the refrigerator in a lidded container.

Feel free to stir in a little extra cream if the crème fraîche gets too thick.

basic salad dressings

I'm always surprised when my simple salad dressings are met with oohs and ahhs. Honestly, there's not much to my concoctions, which just goes to show how much better homemade dressing tastes than any bottled variety. Plus, when you make your own dressing, you know you're not pouring any weird chemicals or preservatives onto your healthy veg!

These are our two house dressings. Mustardy Balsamic is really our favorite, and it works on nearly every salad: Mixed greens or butter lettuce with a little of this stuff is quite good, and any green salad with fruit like apples, pears, or persimmons is great. The Citrus Garlic Dressing is one I'll use on arugula, with radishes, jicama, and other fresh, bright, crisp veggies. A few spoonfuls of the lemony dressing can also brighten up a pot of beans.

Making dressing was one of the first kitchen tasks I taught my kids. Both of them can whip together a dressing without a bit of fuss, and you can too.

mustardy balsamic dressing
(enough for 2 salads)

⅓–½ cup extra-virgin olive oil

2 tablespoons balsamic vinegar (I like the hint of sweetness it brings to the dressing)

1 heaping teaspoon Dijon mustard

Sea salt

citrus garlic dressing
(enough for 1 or 2 salads)

⅓ cup extra-virgin olive oil

2 tablespoons freshly squeezed lemon juice

1 clove garlic, pressed or finely chopped

Zest of 1 lemon (optional)

Sea salt

The prep for both dressings is the same:

Place all of the dressing ingredients into a lidded jar. Screw on the cover nice and tight. Shake like crazy for 10 seconds. (If you have little ones at home, let them do the shakin'.) Open the jar and you'll have a well-blended, emulsified dressing. Take a leaf of whatever salad greens you plan to eat, and dip it into the dressing to taste for seasoning. Add a little more of this or that, until it tastes just right to you. These dressings are simple templates to get you started. Feel free to doctor and personalize them as much as you wish.

acknowledgments

Elissa Altman, how did I get so lucky as to get you as my editor? Thank you for your intelligence, passion, and deeply soulful approach to food. I couldn't have asked for a more nurturing shepherd for this project, and I only hope we'll get to make many more books together.

To Carole Bidnick, amazing agent and wonderful friend, thanks for being "over the moon" and for finding such a perfect home for me and this book.

To Rodale Books and the entire Rodale family: 30 years ago, J. I. Rodale inspired my mom to plant a massive organic garden. Thankfully, those home-grown flavors remain emblazoned on my tastebuds. To Kara Plikaitis and the rest of the fantastic team at Rodale, thank you for taking such good care of me.

Alexandra Penney, thank you for boundless enthusiasm and inspiration. You gave me a real kick in the pants to get serious about my proposal and make this book happen. You promised I would love authoring a book, and you were completely right.

Abby Turin and Jonathan Gans, thanks for your friendship, for cooking so many tasty meals together, and for being willing to spend weeks on end being gluten-free with me. Thanks to Rachel Cauntay, Justin Cauntay, Amy Frey, and Doug Frey for always being game to grub, and for decades of friendship.

Thanks to Phyllis Grant, for your support, friendship, and marathon Friday phone chats. And to Shoshana Berger, for your early confidence in me (and Yummy Supper) and for introducing me to the generous Leslie Jonath.

To my army of dedicated, hard-working, talented recipe testers who have yet to be thanked above: Ann Messana, Rich Price, Caitlin Patterson, Julie Kim Beal, Meg McDowell, Megan Burnham, Barbara Scott, Babette Sange, Marites Abeug, Holland Lynch, Saya McKenna, Naoko Akiyama, David Katzev, Dana Smith, Stephen Florance, Emma Gardner, Jennifer Sime, Chris Kinney, Sarah Horwich, Andy Spear, Tracy Lenihan, Martin Johnson, Sarah Marchick, Marian Bradley-Kohr, Dave Levin, Caroline Shlain, Anna Gade,

Charlotte Greensit, Alexandra Engs, Ariel Trost, Mary Goglio, Whitney Roberson, JP Daughton, and Justine Milani. Your feedback and insights were crucial in making these recipes sing.

To Mini, Pip, Donna, Sujatha, and Eurydice (and Aunt Nita, of course), thank you for sharing your beautiful recipes with all of us.

To Josh Vogel and Kelly Zaneto at Blackcreek Mercantile & Trading Co. Your extraordinary cutting boards and hand-carved kitchen tools make cooking even more dreamy. Thanks to Trish Baldwin for keeping our kitchen stocked in delectable Stonehouse Olive Oil.

A massive thanks to all of you who read and cook from Yummy Supper. Thank you for sharing your time and talents and for opening your kitchens to me.

To my dad, for first placing a camera in my hands, teaching me to see beauty, and making a mean Caesar—thank you.

Mom, you started me on this path and continue to inspire me in my kitchen and garden every day. Thank you for giving me this huge gift.

Otis and Lilah, I am grateful to be your mom—you bring me endless joy and keep me determined to cook food that makes your bellies happy. Our times spent cooking together and sitting around the table are some of the best moments of my life. (If only we could work a little on our manners, and stop eating everything with our fingers!)

Paul, my love, the person I most enjoy being with in the kitchen—thank you for being eternally patient, encouraging, and always game to chop. I feel beyond lucky that we get to cook so many more meals together.

index

Boldfaced page references indicate photographs.